Table of Contents

About the Author i
Introduction 1
How to Tune Your Guitar 2
Lesson 1: Strumming & Reading Rhythms 5
Lesson 2: How to Read a Fretboard Diagram 8
      The Fastest Way to Learn Chords 10
      A Quick Lesson in Music Theory 11
Lesson 3: G Major & E Minor 12
Lesson 4: D7 Chord 15
Lesson 5: C Major & A Minor 18
      Common Chord Progressions 21
Lesson 6: D Major & A7 25
Lesson 7: Eighth Note Strumming 28
Lesson 8: A Major & E7 33
Lesson 9: E Major & B7 38
Lesson 10: D Minor 44
Lesson 11: G7 49
Lesson 12: Introducing Barre Chords 57
Lesson 13: 3/4 Time 61
Lesson 14: B♭ Major & C7 66
Lesson 15: Introducing Minor Barre Chords 71
Lesson 16: B Minor & C Minor 74
Lesson 17: Ties & Rests 77
Lesson 18: F♯ Minor 84
Lesson 19: Introducing Suspended Chords 87
Lesson 20: Esus4 & Fsus4 91
Chord Reference 104

About the Author

Christian J. Triola holds a Bachelor's Degree in Music (Jazz Studies) and a Master's Degree in Education, both from The University of Akron. He has taught guitar, bass, mandolin, ukulele, and piano for over 15 years, published over a dozen guitar method books, and has played in a variety of bands in addition to his many solo performances.

What is the Missing Method?

The Missing Method for Guitar is the guitar method imprint of Tenterhook Books, LLC, owned and operated by Christian J. Triola and his wife, Amy Joy Triola. The imprint began in 2013 in an effort to bring method books that didn't exist to Christian's guitar students. Today, we have expanded that mission to create high quality instructional materials that inspire and empower all levels of guitar player, from absolute beginners to professional guitarists.

The Missing Method now spans many series of guitar books, addressing topics from chords, to note reading, practice strategies, playing techniques and much more. Learn more at TheMissingMethod.com.

Introduction

How this book works

This book is designed to take you step by step through the process of learning how to strum a guitar using the most commonly played chords. Everyone from the greatest classical and jazz players to hobbyists in their bedrooms know these chords.

What are chords?

A **chord** is just another way of saying **harmony**. It is a combination of two or more notes played together at the same time. When learning guitar, many people start out by learning chords, while others learn how to read **notation**. Both are just as important, and after a while you'll start to understand the strong relationship between the two.

What you will learn

Each lesson will present you with something new, in small chunks, along with plenty of exercises to help you learn all the chords in this book. Along the way, you'll also learn how to tune your guitar, read chord diagrams, count rhythms, and play common strumming patterns. Also included are practice songs that will teach you how to read sheet music for guitar accompaniment. By the time you've finished this book, you'll have the skills you need to be able to play thousands of songs!

Access the audio files

Audio files are available for each exercise and song. Access these via The Missing Method website: https://themissingmethod.com/audio-files/.

How to Tune Your Guitar

1 The first thing you need to know in order to tune your guitar is what notes to tune to. In music, every different sound is given a name. The pitches are given letter names to make them easy to refer to. They are: A B C D E F G. On the guitar, each string is tuned to a specific pitch so that everything sounds the way it's supposed to. The chart below shows you the pitches of each string.

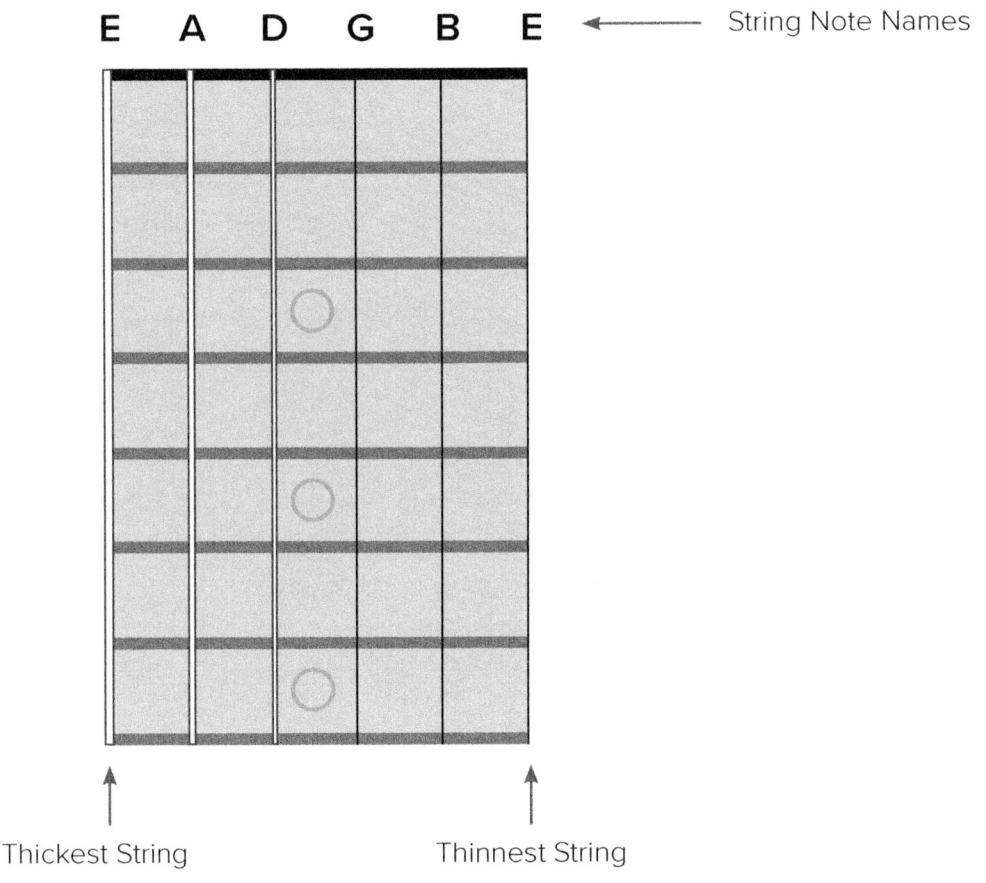

There are a couple of sayings that can help you remember the names of the strings, from thick to thin:

Eddie **A**te **D**ynamite, **G**ood **B**ye **E**ddie.

Or the less violent:

Every **A**mateur **D**oes **G**et **B**etter **E**ventually.

2 The second thing you should know is that tuning takes practice. It can be a little frustrating at first, but once you've done it a few times it gets easier and easier.

3 The third thing you need to know is that most of the time your guitar will only need slight adjustments. Once it's in tune, it will usually stay fairly close to tune most of the time. However, it is recommended that you check your tuning every time you pick up the guitar. Be sure to listen carefully to the sound of an in-tune guitar, so you become familiar with what it should sound like.

4 Now that you know this, we can begin tuning the guitar. There are several tuning methods. The best method is to buy a guitar tuner and learn how to use it. (You can find information on tuners on the next page.)

Typically, most tuners will show which note you are playing and then tell you whether or not the note is too low, too high, or in tune. Usually, a meter of some kind will display this information.

If the string is too low, you'll want to tighten the string by turning it to the left. If the string is too high, you'll want to lower it by turning it to the right. Be sure to listen to the sound of the string as well. Your ear will help you figure out if you are going too far from the in-tune note.

Guitar Tuners

Tuners come in all shapes and sizes. There are credit card sized tuners, apps, and clip-on tuners that attach to your guitar. The best apps for tuning include Pitchlab and GuitarTuna. There are many others that can work as well and most of them are free.

You can also search YouTube for lessons and suggestions on how to get your guitar in tune.

Another way you can tune the guitar is to use a reference pitch from an instrument that is already in tune. Most people use a piano, another in-tune guitar, or a pitch pipe to achieve this. In this case, you simply listen to the reference pitch and then match that pitch on your instrument. This can be difficult for beginners, but can help you to develop a strong ear as well as help you to develop your overall musicianship.

Lesson 1: Strumming & Reading Rhythms

How to hold the pick

1 First, curve the fingers of your picking hand inward, while keeping them relaxed. Don't make a fist.

2 Second, place the pick on top of the first knuckle, so that the point of the pick faces outward.

3 Third, place your thumb over the pick to hold it in place. (See below)

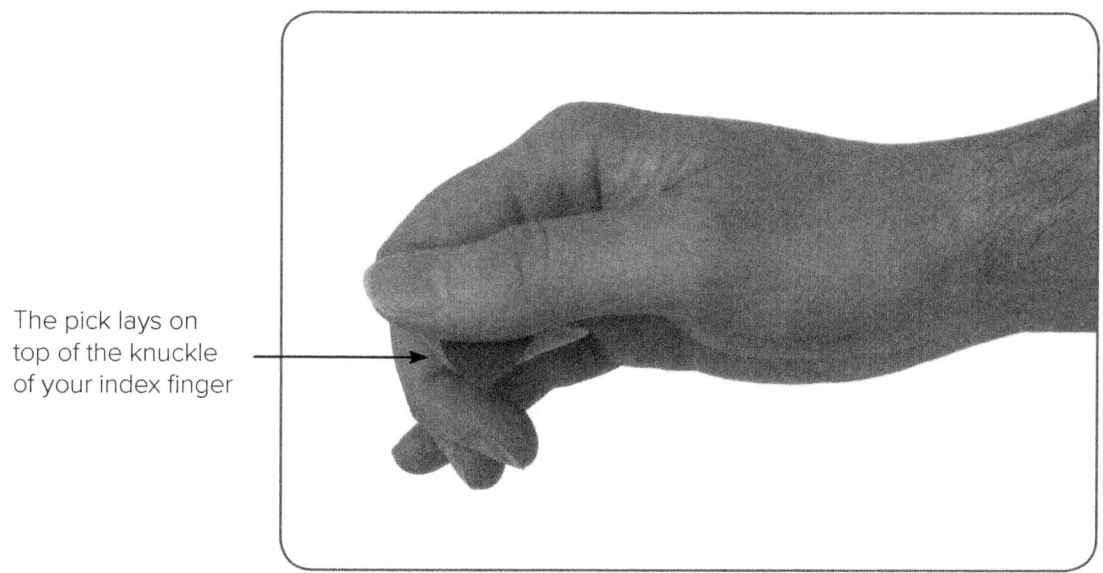

The pick lays on top of the knuckle of your index finger

This may feel awkward or uncomfortable at first, but once you get used to it, you'll have full control over the pick.

How to strum the guitar

When strumming, don't use your whole arm; simply swing from the wrist. To do this, start with your wrist slightly bent upward, then release the pick across the strings in a natural semi-circular motion. Don't force it or overthink it. Just let your picking hand glide over the strings.

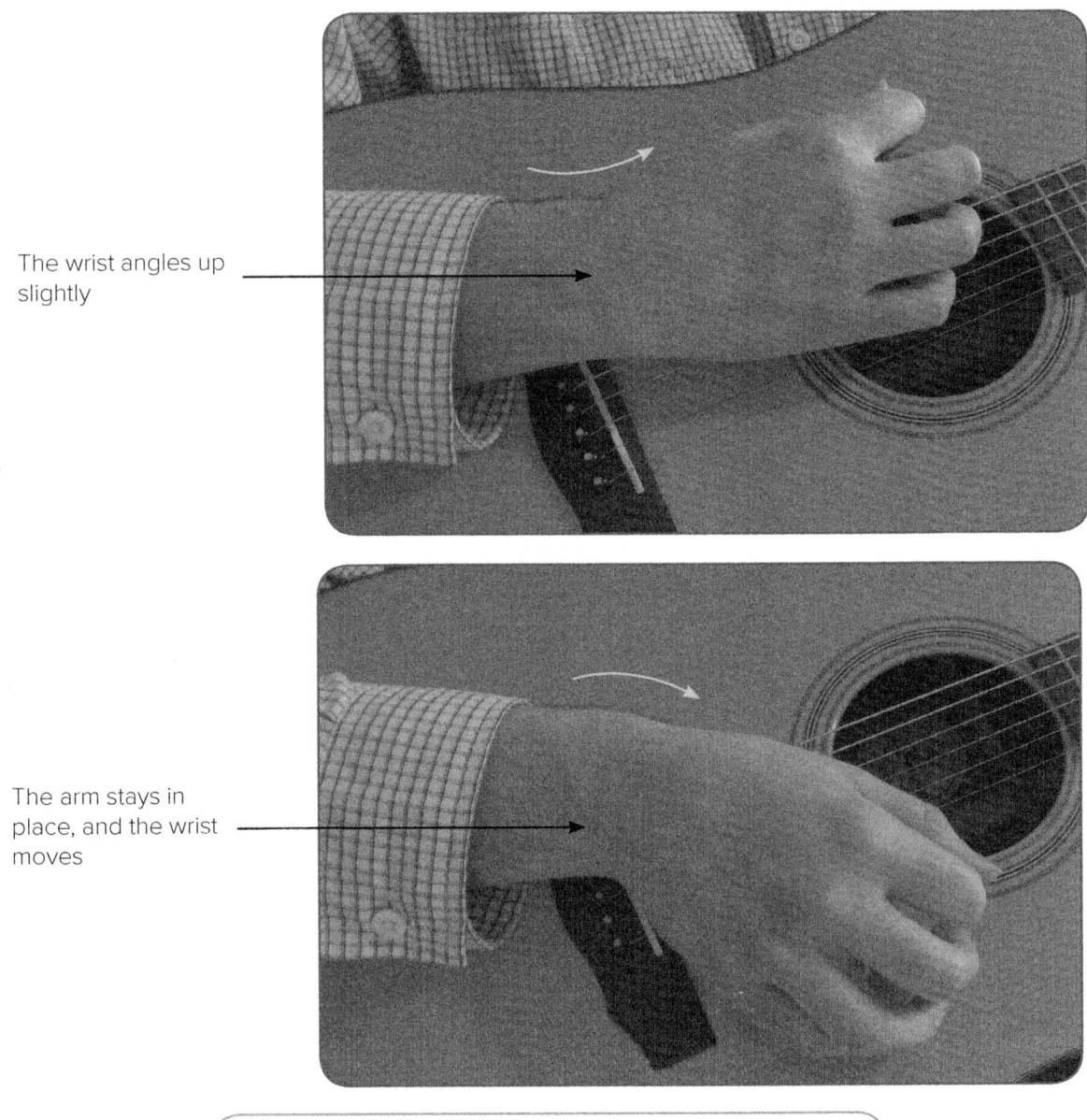

The wrist angles up slightly

The arm stays in place, and the wrist moves

Tip:
It takes a while to develop control over this motion, but in time it will become second nature.

Time

Staff with Treble Clef

The staff (shown above) is divided into sections called **bars** or **measures**. This is done to make the music easier to read.

Each measure is only allowed a certain number of beats. This limitation allows us to keep track of time. The grouping of these beats is called **meter**. The most common meter is four beats per measure, called 4/4 time.

Beat is the underlying current of music. You don't necessarily hear the beat. Think of it as a second hand on a clock, a constant steady clicking that helps you keep track of time.

What you actually play is the **rhythm**. Rhythm tells you how long or how short a pitch or chord should be held. For example, in 4/4 time a whole note (see below) is sustained for four beats. A half note is sustained for two beats. A quarter note (which takes up a quarter of the measure) is sustained for only one beat.

Try it: Practice strumming the following rhythms.

Note: You don't need to know how to read music to play the exercises below. This is called slash notation, and it simply denotes the rhythm, not the pitch.

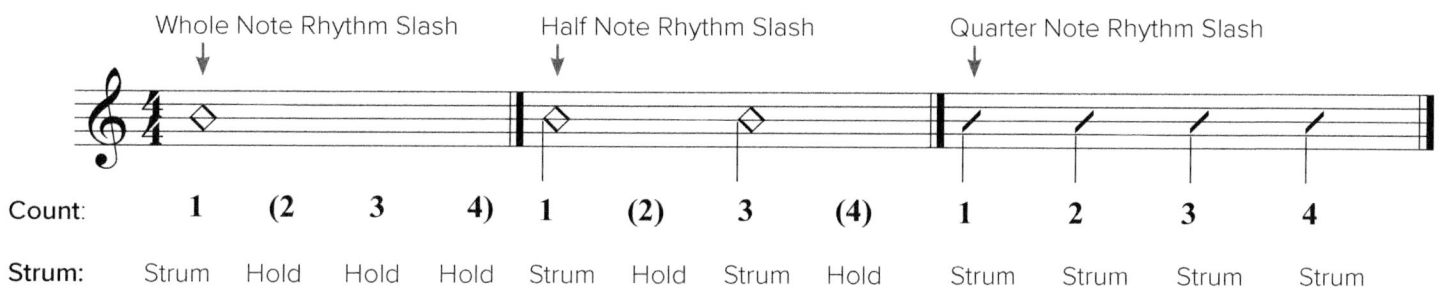

Lesson 2:
How to Read a Fretboard Diagram

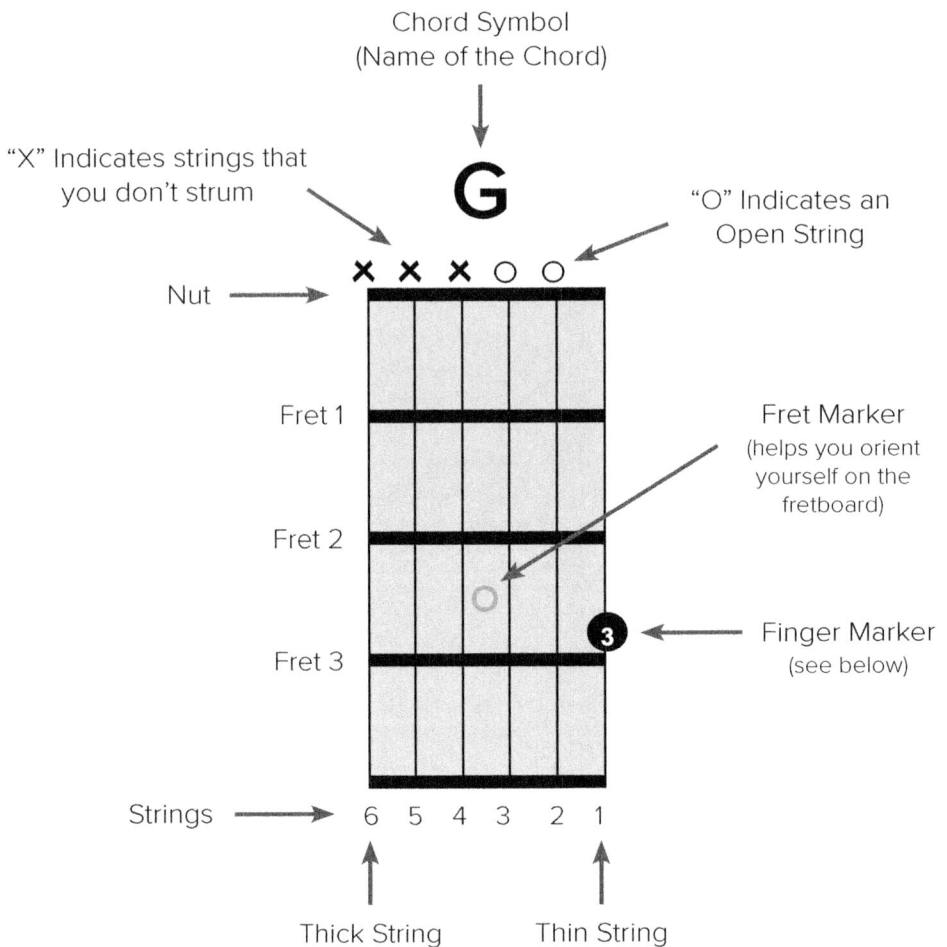

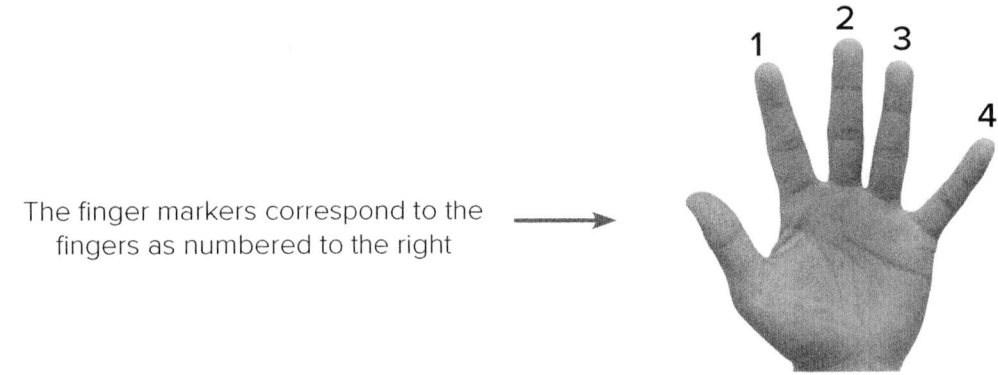

Technique Tip:
When placing fingers on the fretboard, always keep your wrist dropped and your fingers on their tips. Remember only your fingertips and the thumb behind the neck should be touching the guitar. Keep the palm of your hand off the neck. This will help you build finger strength and solid technique.

Try it: Practice strumming using the G chord with the rhythms below.

Rhythm 1:

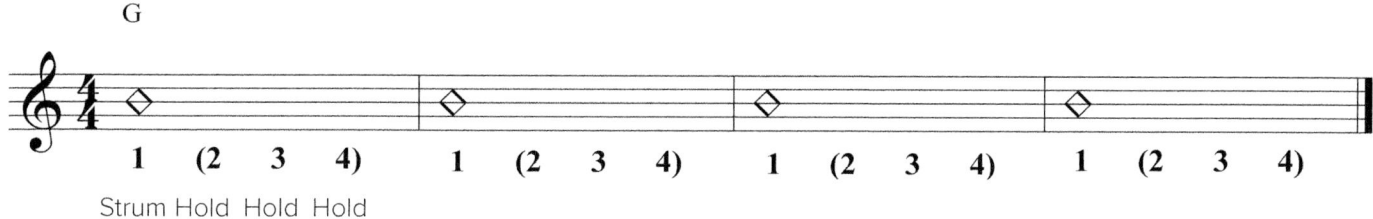

Rhythm 2:

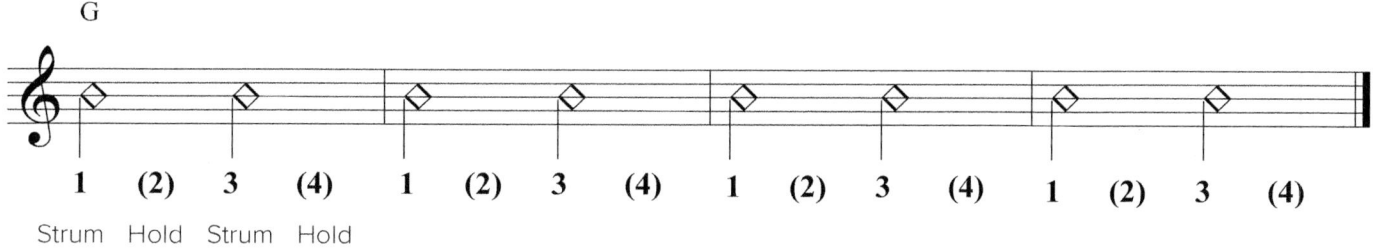

Rhythm 3:

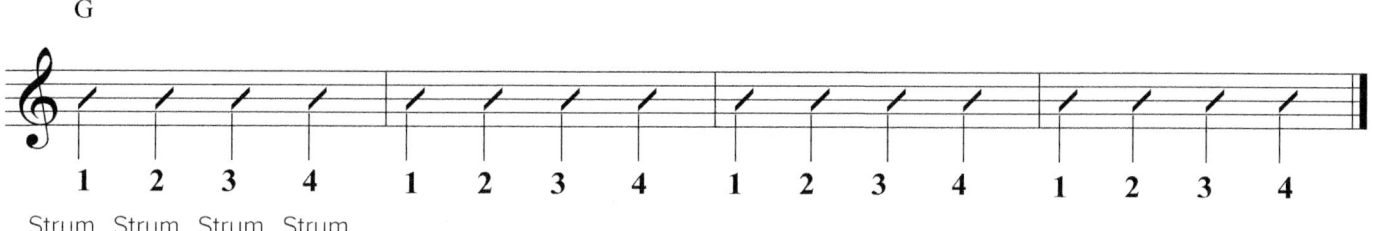

The Fastest Way to Learn Chords

Learning new chords can take time, so the best way I've found to speed up this process is through the use of **visualization**.

1. Place your fingers on the correct notes to form a chord, G for example.

2. Strum the chord to make sure you have it right.

3. Take a moment to memorize the placement of each finger individually. What fret and string is your first finger on, your second, your third, etc? Memorize what it looks like, what it feels like.

4. Once the finger placement is clear in your mind, take your fingers off the fretboard.

5. Look at your empty fretboard, and in your mind visualize where your fingers would be if you were playing the chord, G for example.

6. Now place your fingers back on the fretboard all at once. Don't place the fingers one at a time. Think of it as a shape, as a whole, rather than a series of finger placements. If your fingers don't quite make it, correct them. Then try again.

Do this as often as necessary. Some chords will come to you easier than others.

A Note About Changing Chords

Changing from chord to chord takes time and practice. So just be patient with yourself if you can't get the chords to change quickly enough right away. This happens to everybody who picks up a guitar. But if you stick with it, you'll soon sound just like you want to.

A Quick Lesson in Music Theory

Major, Minor, & Dominant Seven Chords

In music, any combination of pitches is considered a chord, so there are as many chords as there are combinations of sounds. Despite this seemingly endless number of possible combinations, most of them boil down to three primary types: **major**, **minor**, and **dominant seven**.

These labels refer to the sound the chord makes. So you could say a major chord sounds major, a minor chord sounds minor, etc. When comparing the qualities of these chords, major is often described as having a bright sound, minor sounds lower and darker than major, and dominant seven sounds like a more unstable version of major. These three sounds are the basis for a countless number of songs.

Chord Symbols

Throughout the book, you will be learning major, minor, and dominant seven chords. When a chord is major, it will be shown by a single letter name (Ex: G). When a chord is minor, there will be a lowercase "m" next to the letter (Ex: Gm). The dominant seven chords will have the number 7 next to them (Ex: G7). These combinations of letters and numbers are called **chord symbols**.

Lesson 3: G Major & E Minor

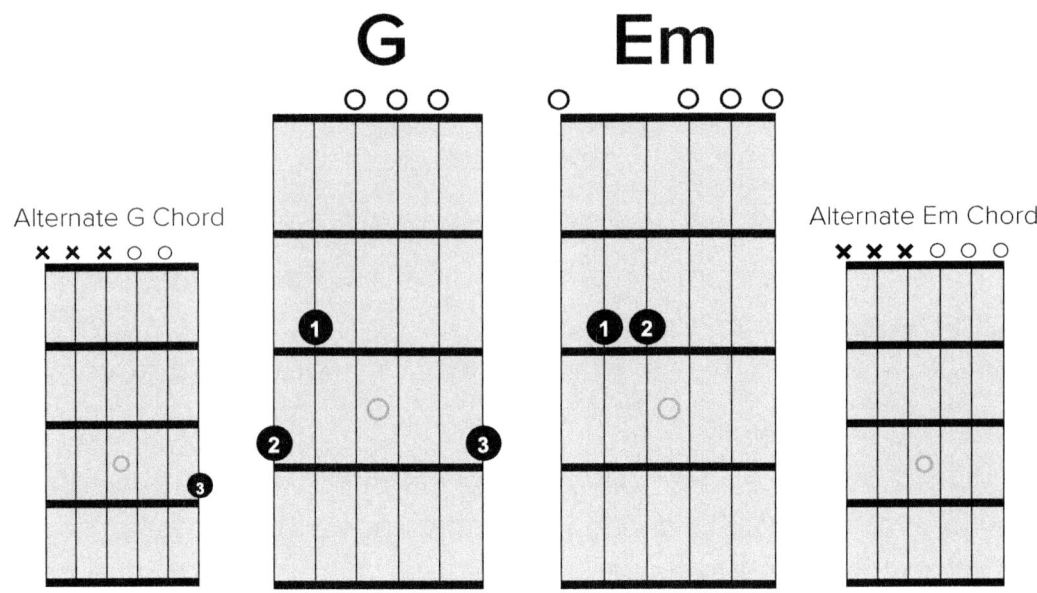

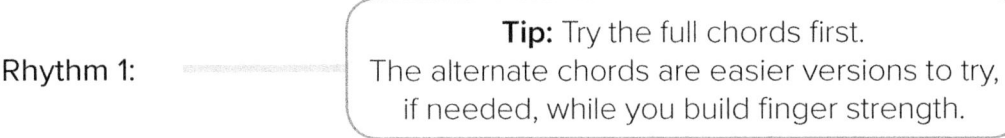

Try it: Practice the G major and E minor chords using the rhythms below.

Rhythm 1:

Tip: Try the full chords first. The alternate chords are easier versions to try, if needed, while you build finger strength.

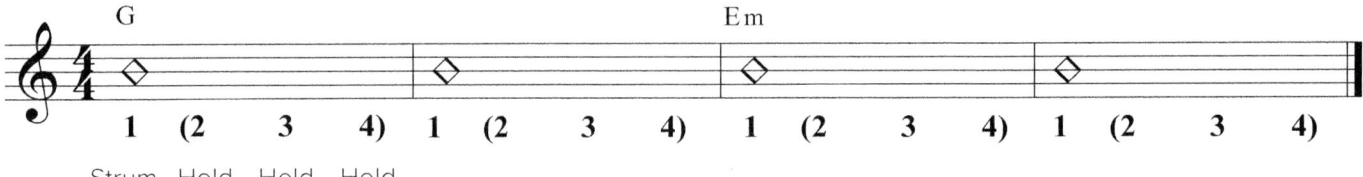

Rhythm 2:

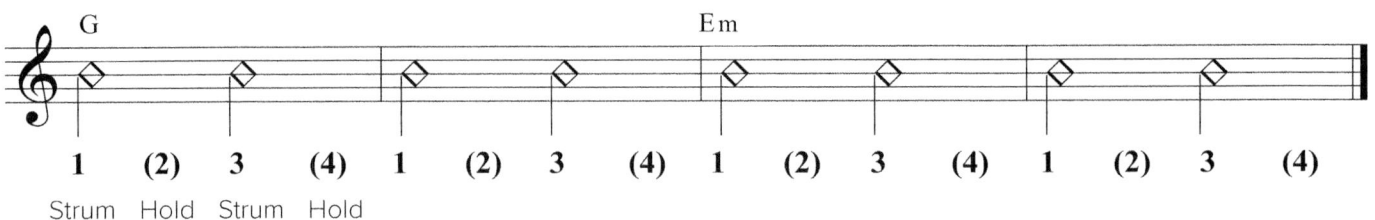

Rhythm 3:

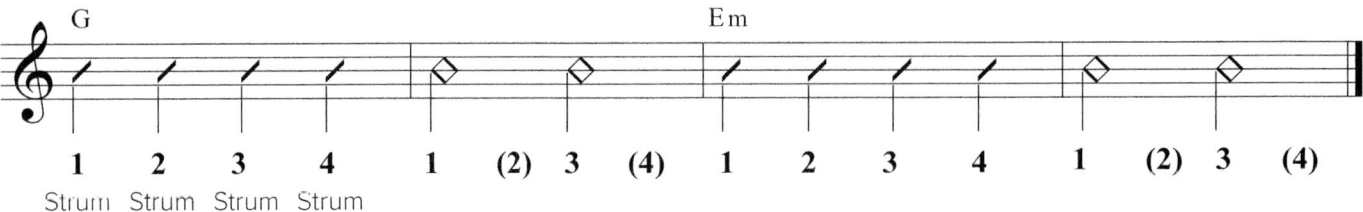

Practicing G and Em

Exercise 1: Strum the E minor chord. Do not pause or stop between measures, keep strumming clearly and evenly.

Exercise 2: Strum the G major and E minor chords.
Note: changing from chord to chord takes time at first, so be patient.

Tip: When changing from G to Em keep your first finger in place, then move your second finger from the last string to the fourth string. This will make changing between these chords easier.

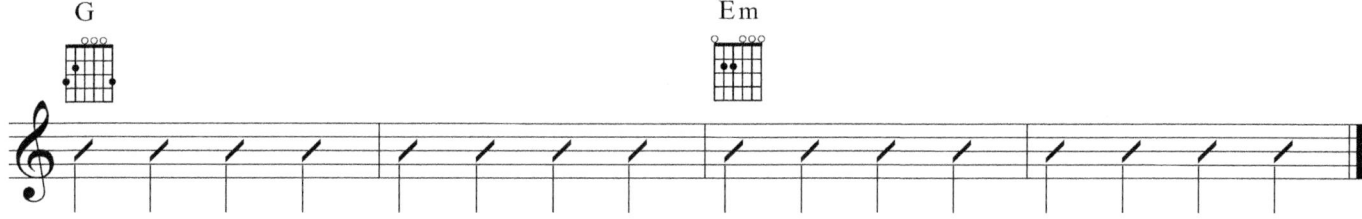

Exercise 3: Strum each chord four times evenly. Don't rush; make sure each strum is the same length as the last.

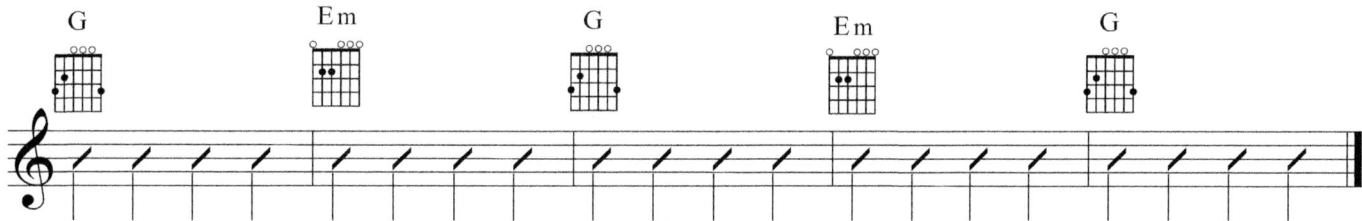

Exercise 4: In measures one and three, strum each chord twice.

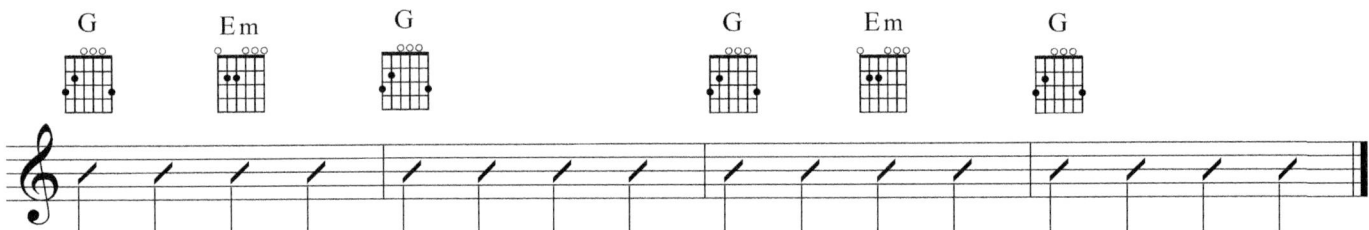

Exercise 5: Strum the Em and G chords. Be sure to go on to line two. The song doesn't end until the double bar line.

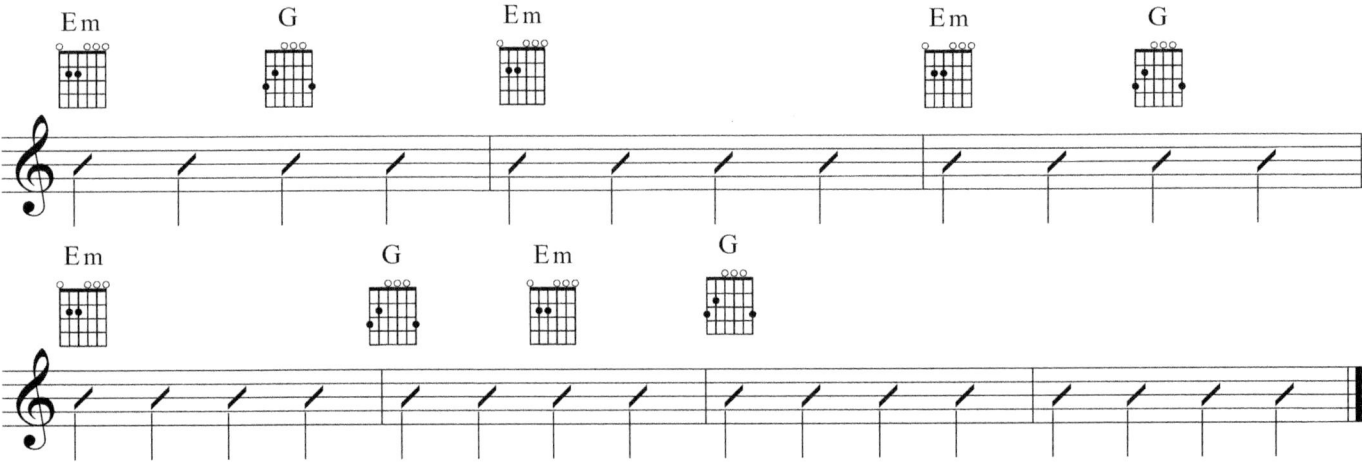

Be sure to review these exercises at least once a day, and make sure you take the time to memorize each chord before moving on to the next set.

Lesson 4:
D7 Chord

D7

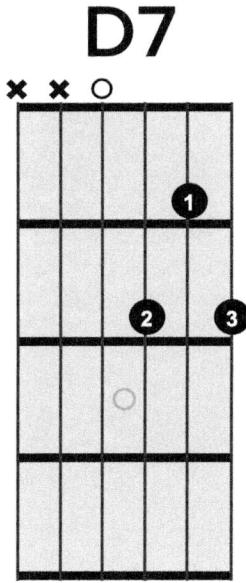

Try it: Practice the D7 chord below using the three different rhythms shown.

Note: Only strum strings 1-4 on this chord. The last two strings (the thickest strings) are not part of the chord (as indicated by the x's above the strings on the chord diagram above).

Tip:
Go slowly at first. Give your mind time to process everything. Also, be sure to fully memorize the chord shape and fingering.

Rhythm 1:

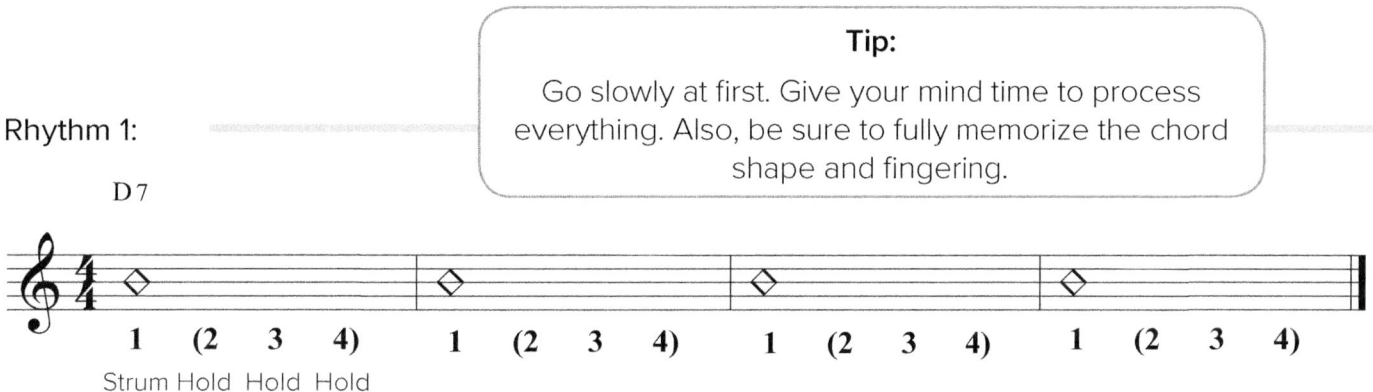

Rhythm 2:

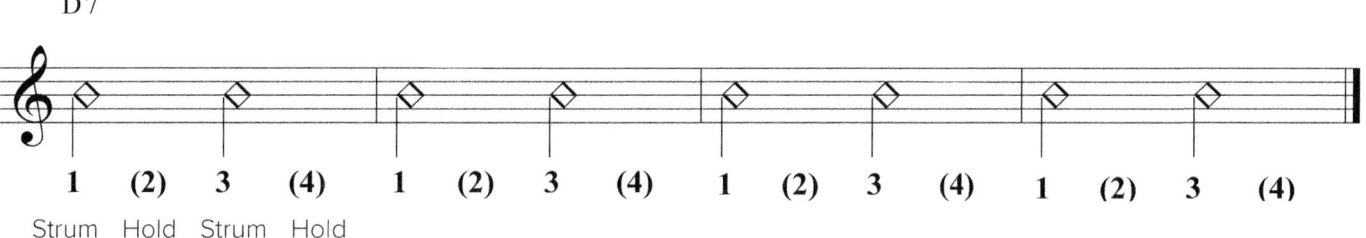

Rhythm 3:

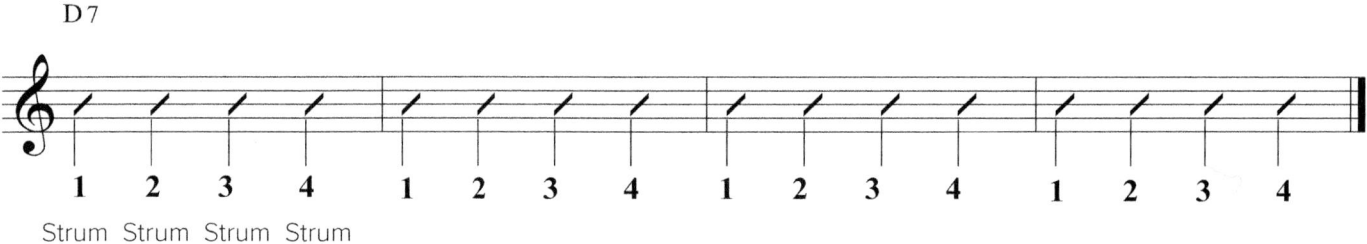

Practicing D7

Exercise 1: Strum the D7 chord followed by the G chord.

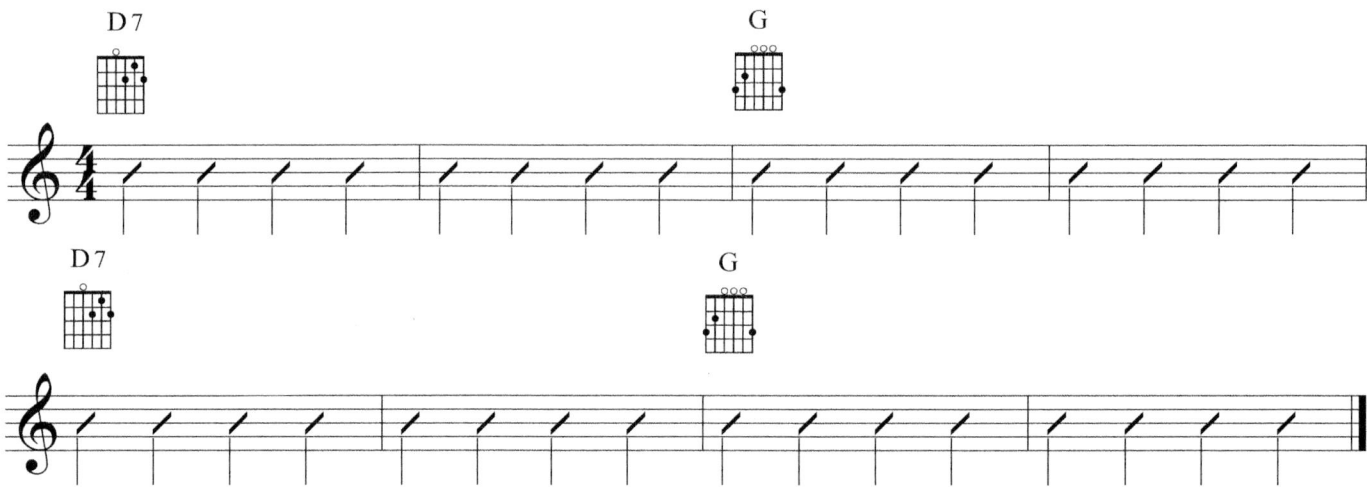

Exercise 2: Strum each chord four times evenly.

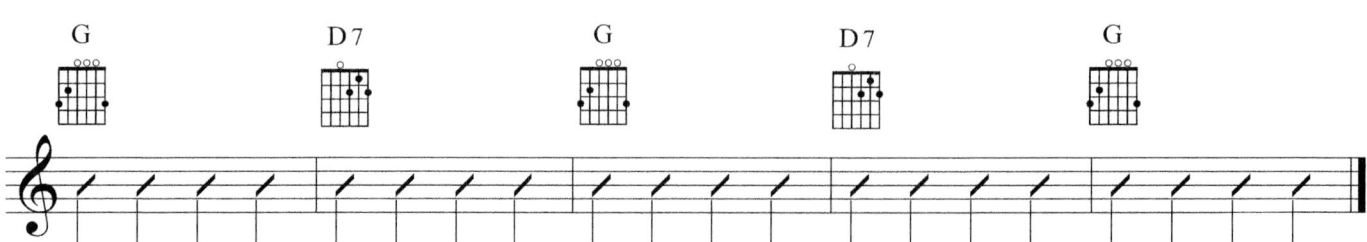

Exercise 3: Strum the following two line exercise.

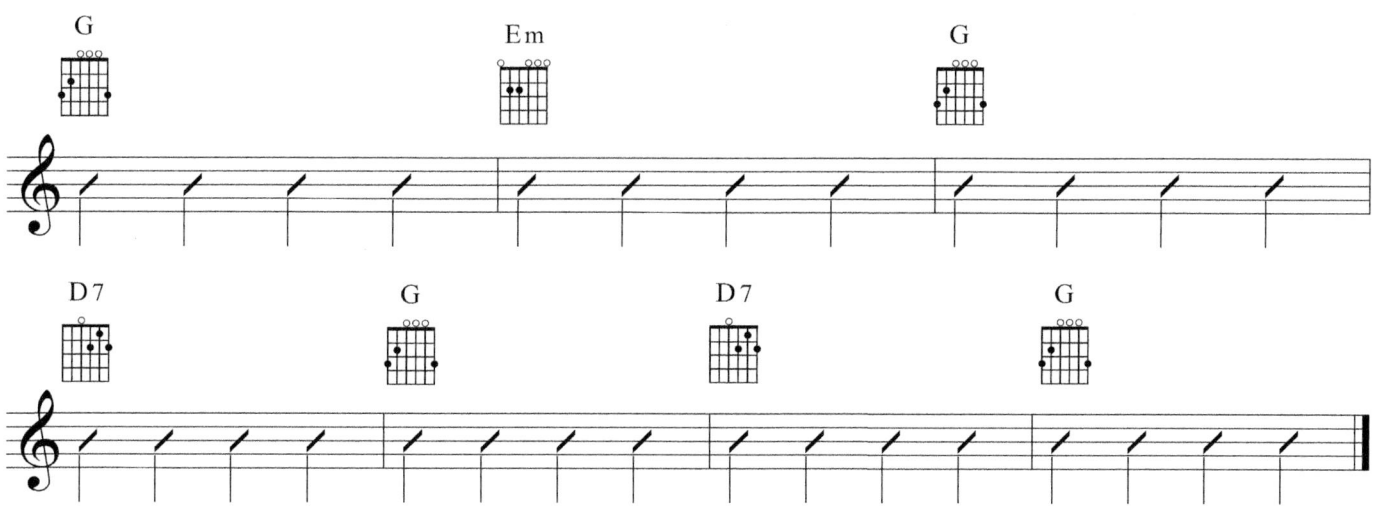

Exercise 4: Strum the following chords.

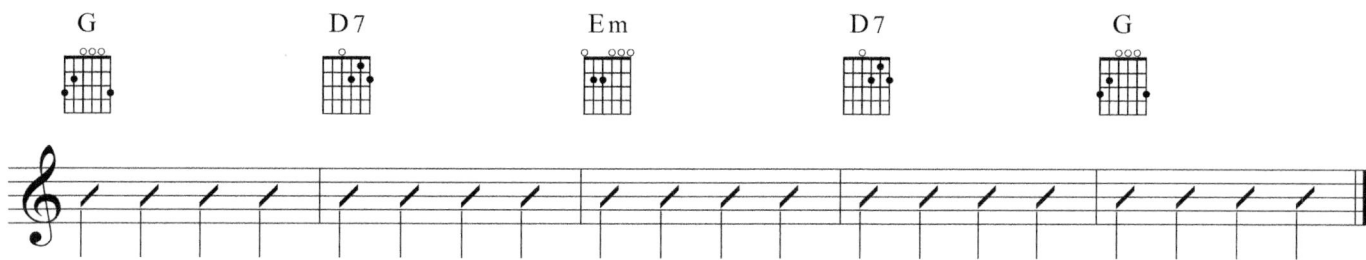

Lesson 5:
C Major & A Minor

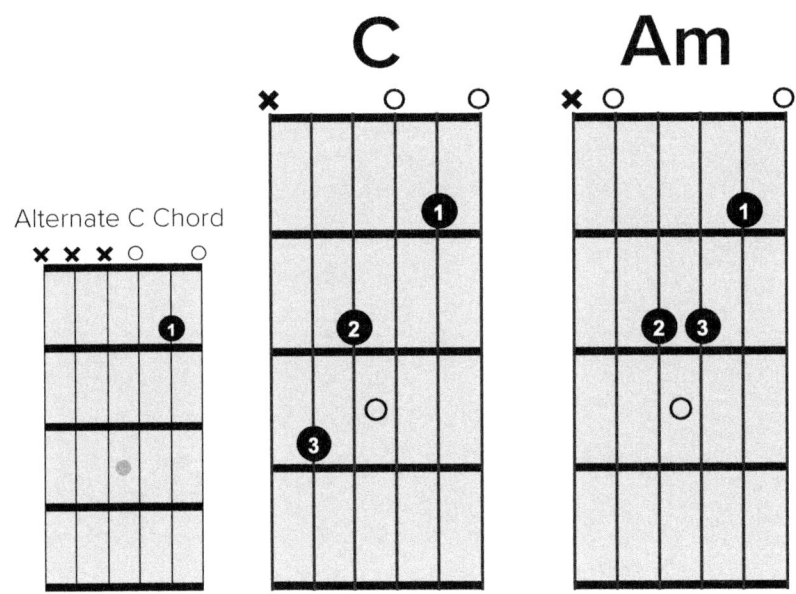

Try it: Practice the C chord below using the indicated strum patterns.

Note that for both of these chords you don't strum the last string (the thick string).

Rhythm 1:

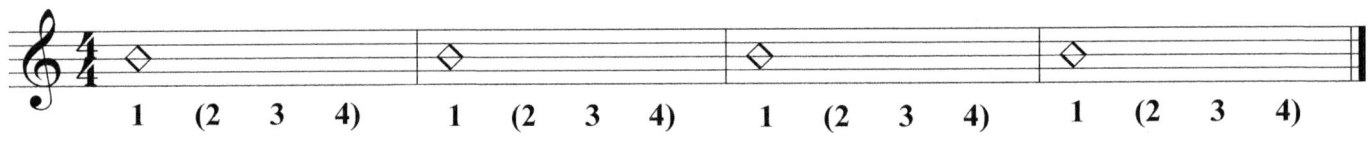

Strum Hold Hold Hold

Rhythm 2:

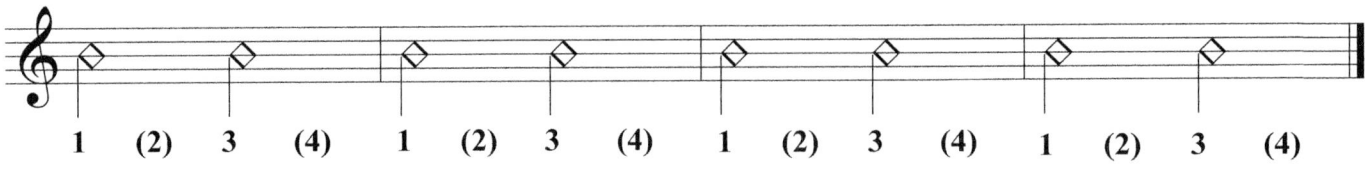

Strum Hold Strum Hold

Rhythm 3:

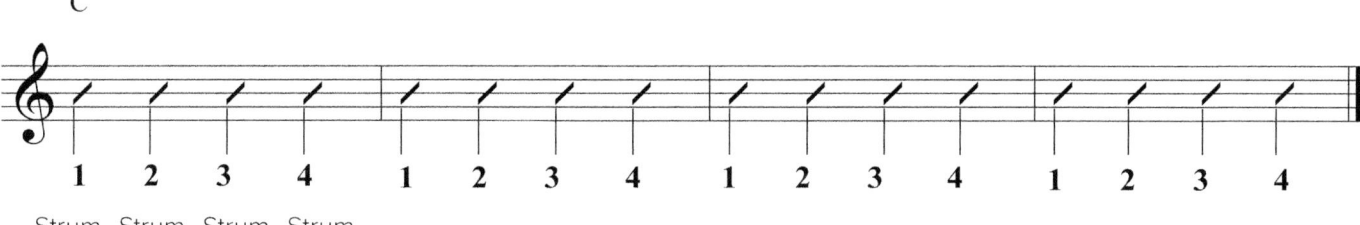

Practicing C and Am

Exercise 1: Strum the A minor chord.

Exercise 2: Strum the C and Am chords.

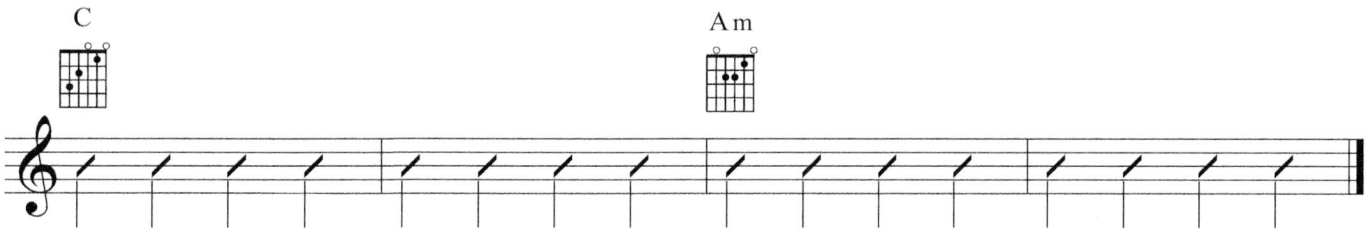

Exercise 3: Strum each chord four times.

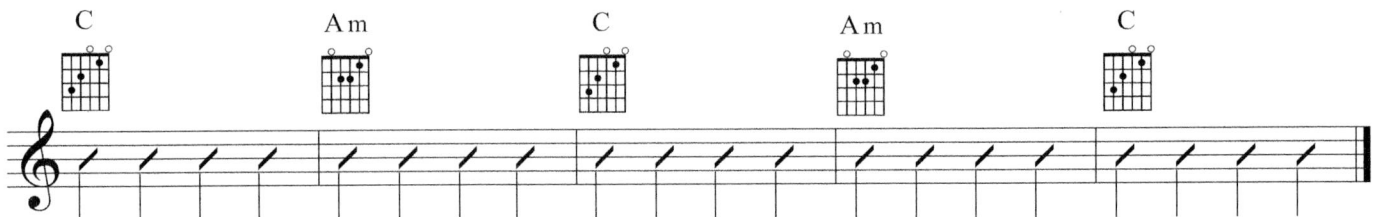

Exercise 4: In measures one and three strum each chord only two times.

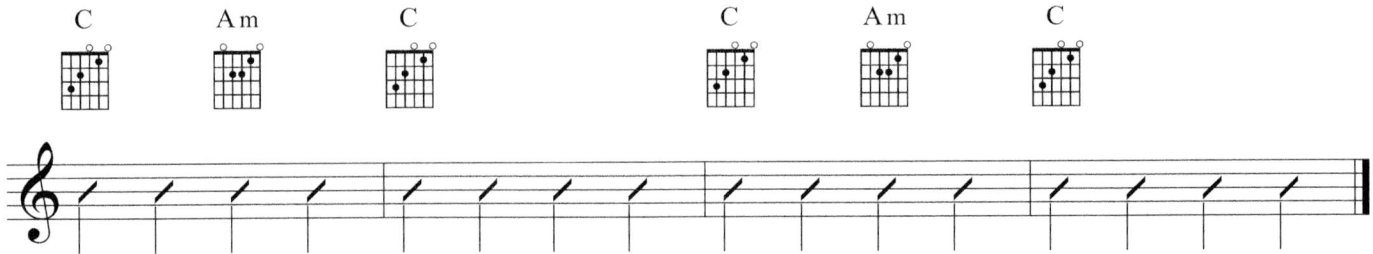

Exercise 5: Strum the C and Am chords in this two line song.

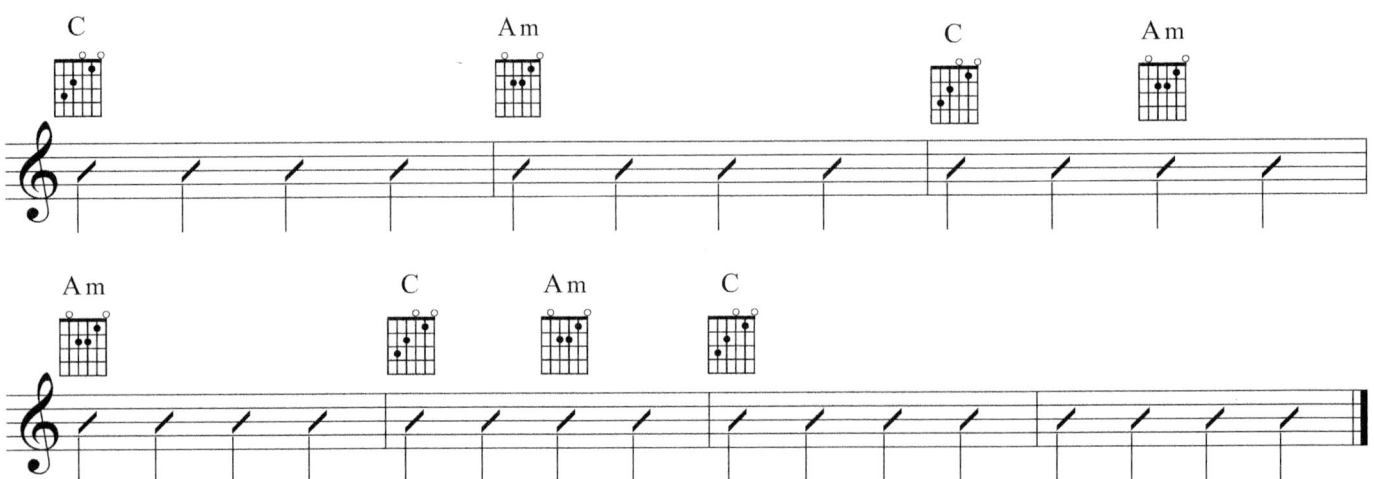

Review: G, Em, D7, C & Am
Using Common Chord Progressions

A **chord progression** refers to a series of chords and the sequence in which they are played. The next several chord progressions are the basis of thousands of popular songs.

Chord Progression 1: Note the half note rhythms in each measure.

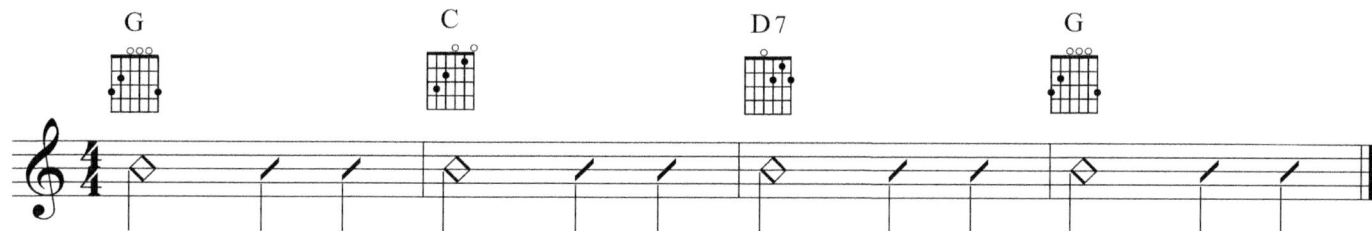

Chord Progression 2: Note the half notes in the final measure.

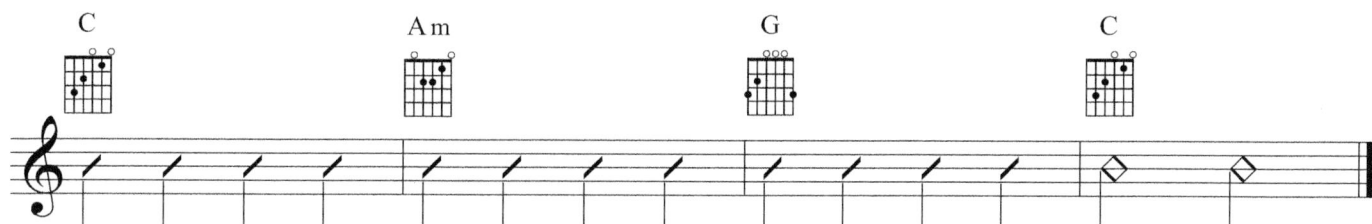

Chord Progression 3: The following progression is often called a turnaround chord progression and is the basis of countless songs.

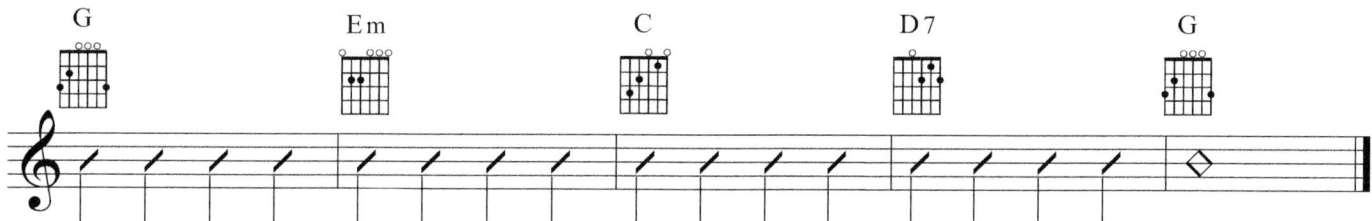

Chord Progression 4: Note the rhythm change in measure 3.

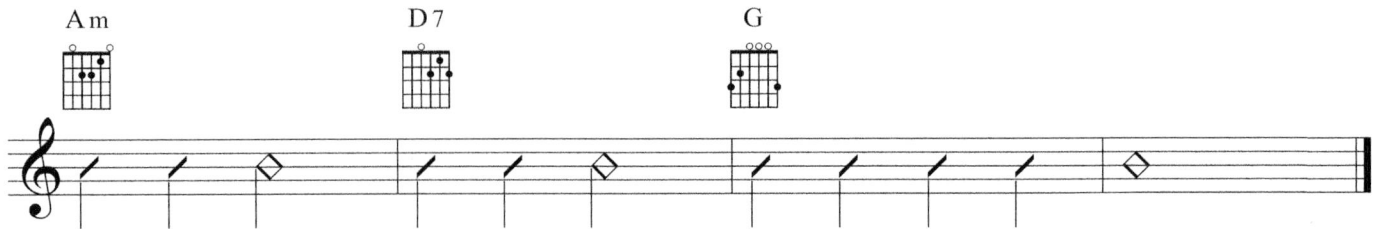

Chord Progression 5: This three line progression is called the **twelve bar blues**. As its name suggests, it originated with the blues and has been adapted to just about every style of music since.

> **Tip:**
> Even though it may seem easy to strum the G chord 16 times in the first line, it can be easy to lose track. Therefore, it is recommended that you count out loud as you strum.

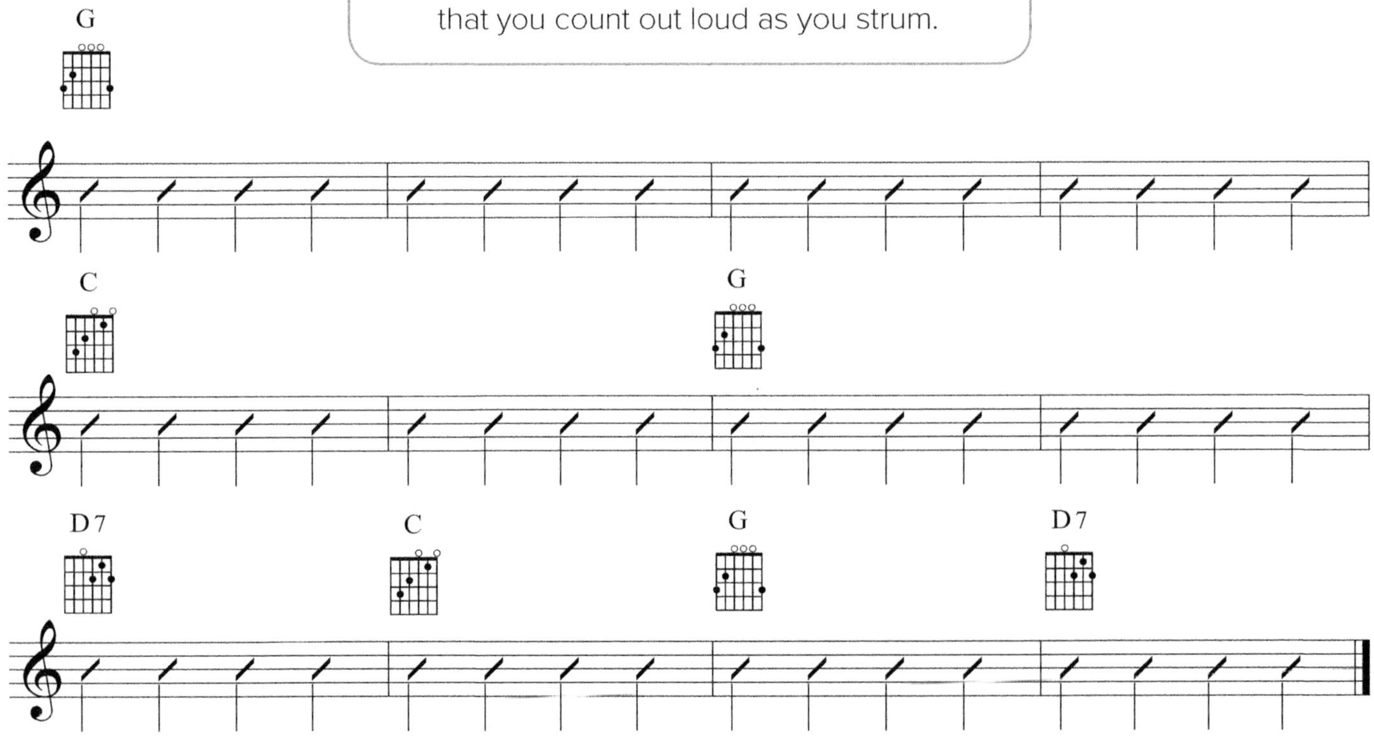

Song Form

On the next page, you'll get a chance to strum through a full song. Every song can be broken down into different sections. The first two most common sections are **verse** and **chorus**. This is done to aid memory, as well as to be able to refer to different parts of the song for rehearsal.

On top of that, a verse and a chorus will normally be different from each other; oftentimes, they will contrast in a variety of ways. The verse usually builds up to the chorus, and then the chorus brings your ear back to the verse. This is repeated until the song comes to an end.

> **Tip:**
> The next song does not include chord diagrams. This is a common practice in many publications and websites, so it is always best to memorize the chord shapes.

Sunrise

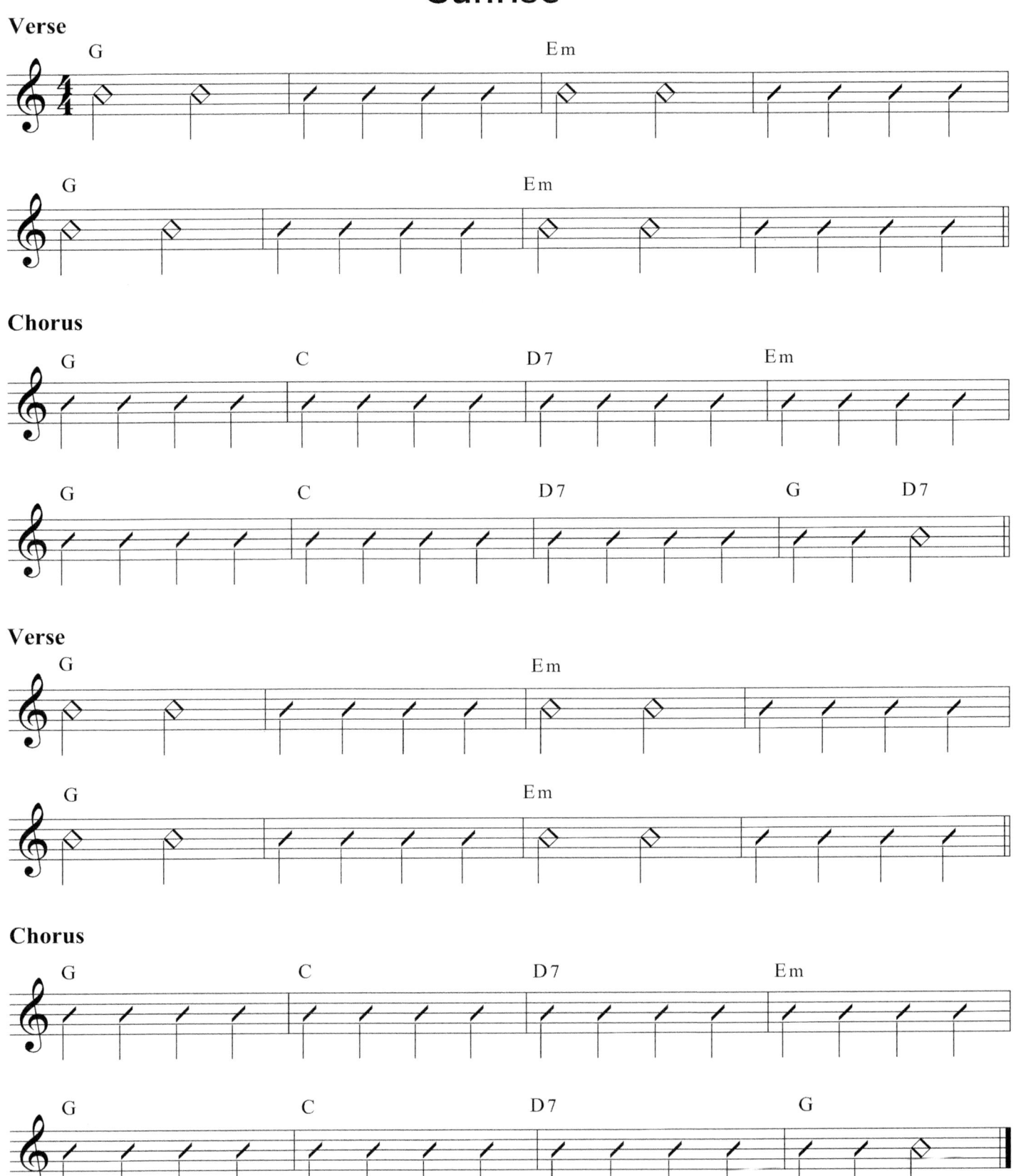

Lesson 6: D Major & A7

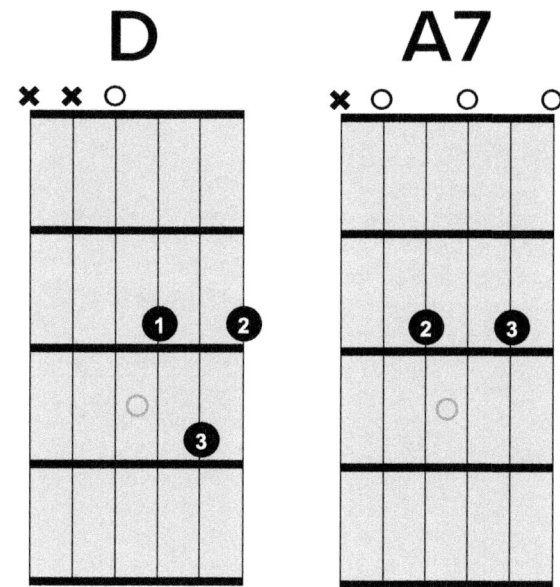

Try it: Practice both the D and A7 chords below using the indicated rhythms.

Rhythm 1:

Tip: Note that the D chord only uses four strings and the A7 uses five.

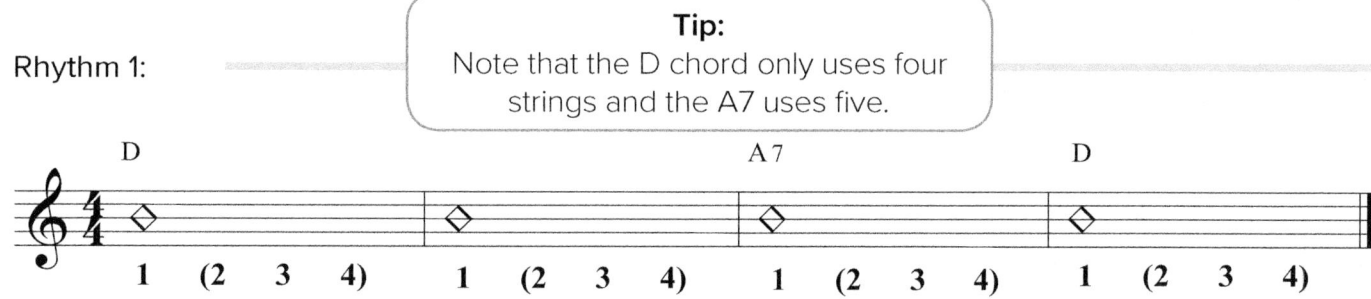

Rhythm 2:

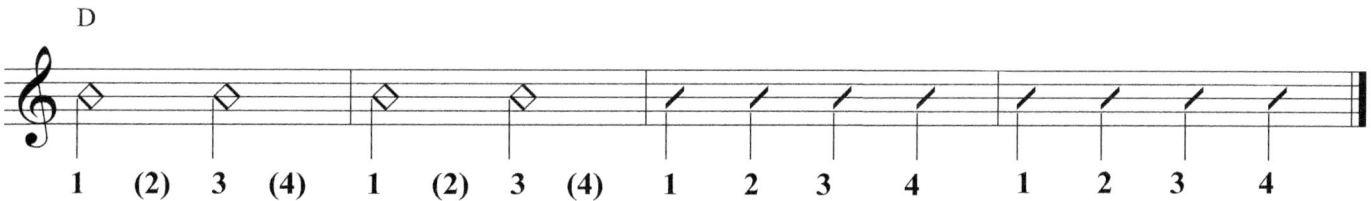

Rhythm 3:

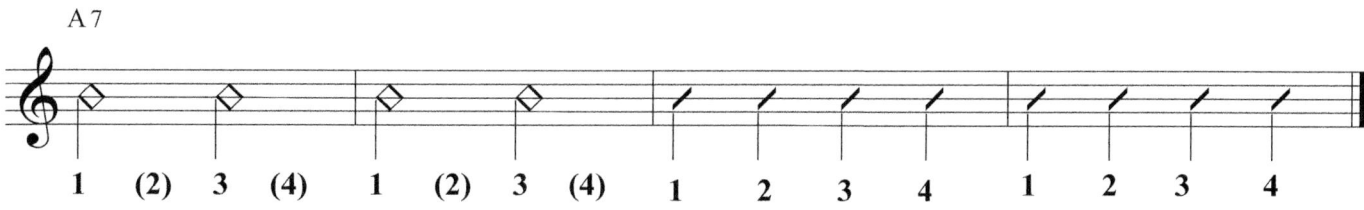

Practicing D, A7, and G

Exercise 1: Practice the D major chord below.

Exercise 2: Practice the A7 chord.

Exercise 3: Practice both the D and A7 chords.

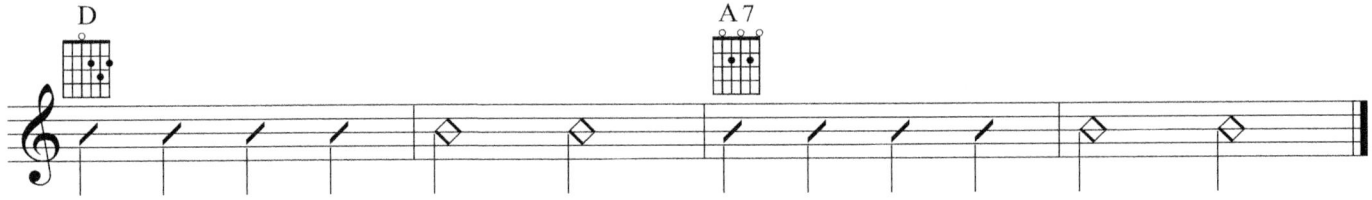

Exercise 4: Strum the D and A7 chords, four per measure.

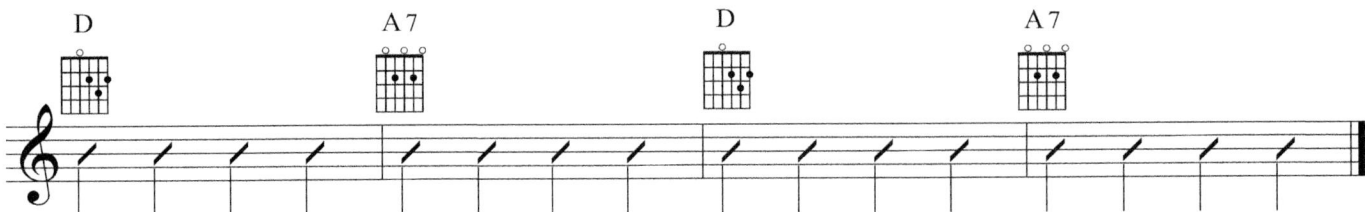

Exercise 5: Note that the G chord has been added to this progression. Also, be sure to pay attention to the changes in rhythm.

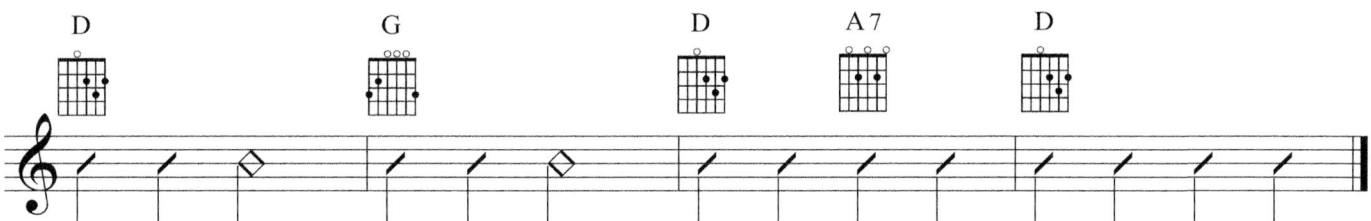

Exercise 6: Strum the D, A7, and G chords in this two line progression.

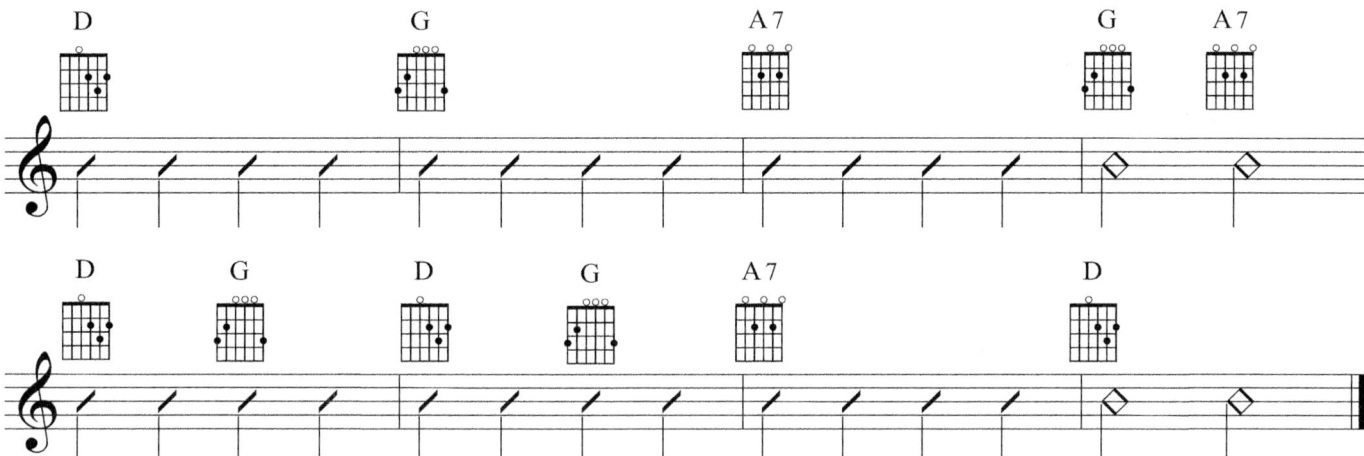

Lesson 7: Eighth Note Strumming

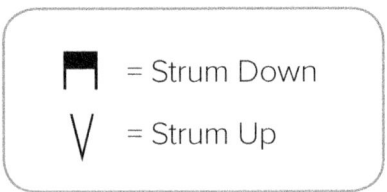

Step 1: Quarter Note Strum Review

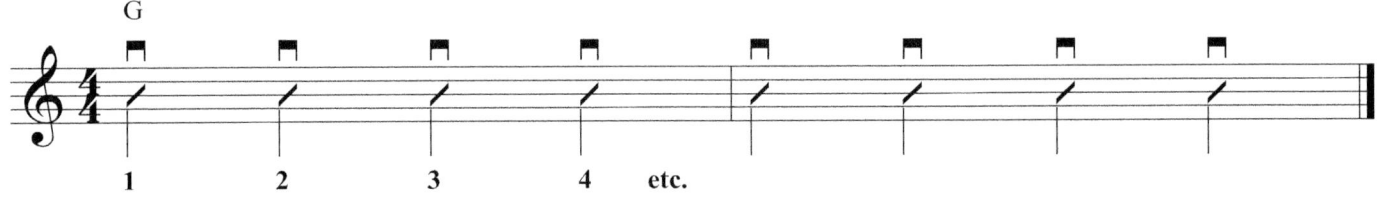

In the above example, each quarter note strum represents one full beat. We can divide each one of those beats in half. When this is done, the resulting notes are called **eighth notes**.

When strumming eighth notes, you strum the first half of the beat downward and the second half of each beat upward. (See Step 2).

Step 2: Eighth Note Strums

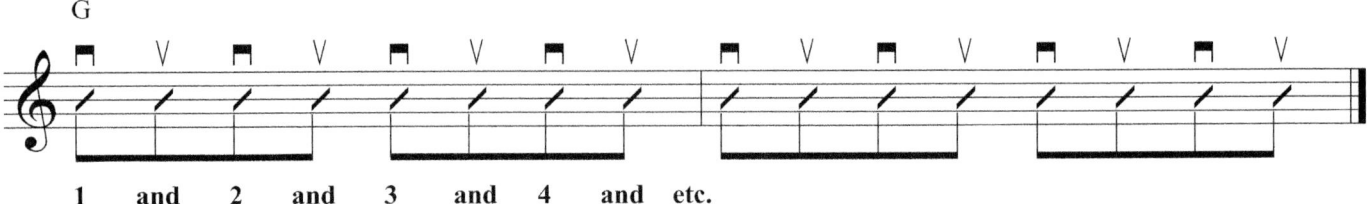

Step 3: Combining Quarter and Eighth Note Strumming

Exercise 1:

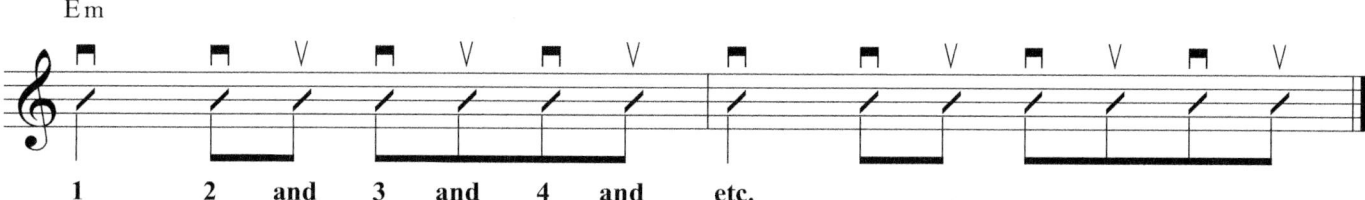

Exercise 2:

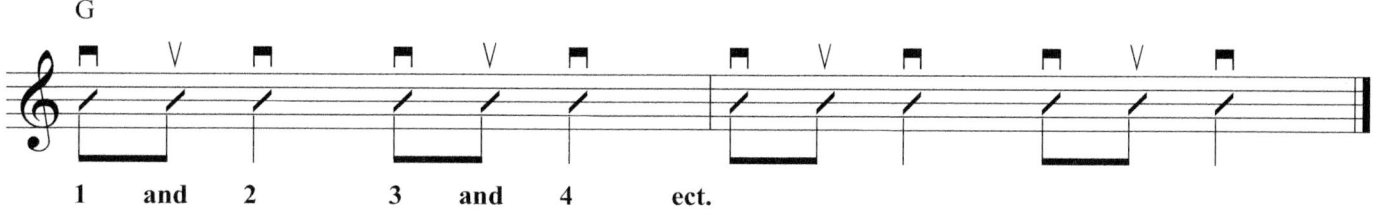

The Repeat Sign

The **repeat sign**, seen in the final measure of the next example, simply tells you to play it again. In example 1, the repeat sign at the beginning shows you where to repeat back to. However, if the composer wants you to repeat the entire song, then no additional repeat sign is used. (See example 2.)

Example 1:

Tip: The repeat sign at the beginning tells you where to repeat back to. It won't always be at the beginning of the song, as it is below.

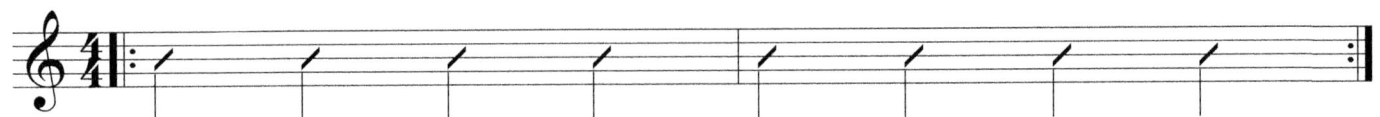

Example 2:

Tip: The repeat sign at the end of a song (as in the exercise below) tells you to repeat the entire song.

Practicing Strumming with Repeat Signs

The next three exercises combine quarter strums with eighth strums and repeat signs.

Exercise 1:

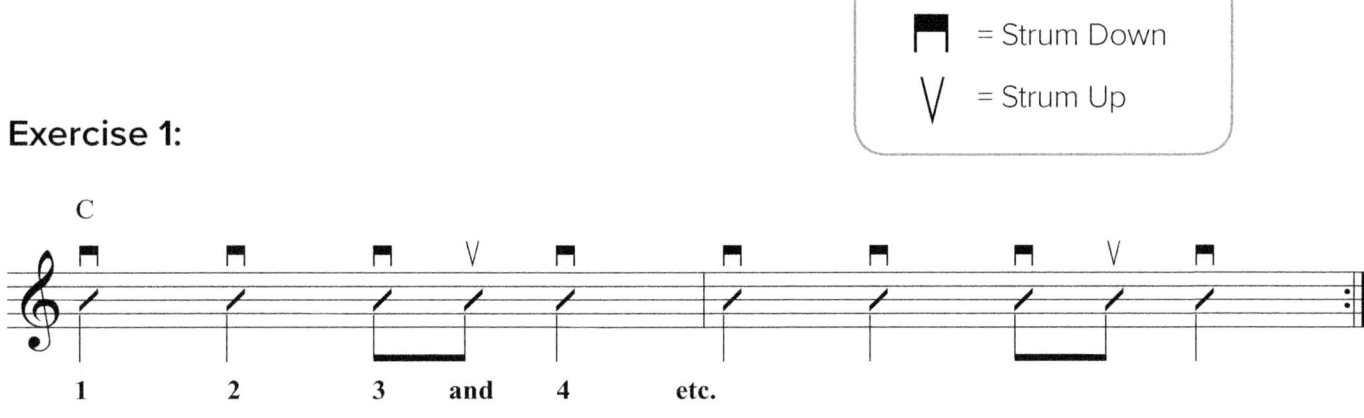

Exercise 2:

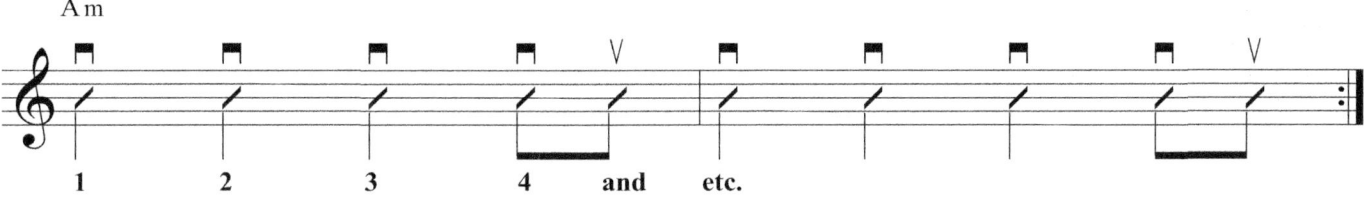

Exercise 3:

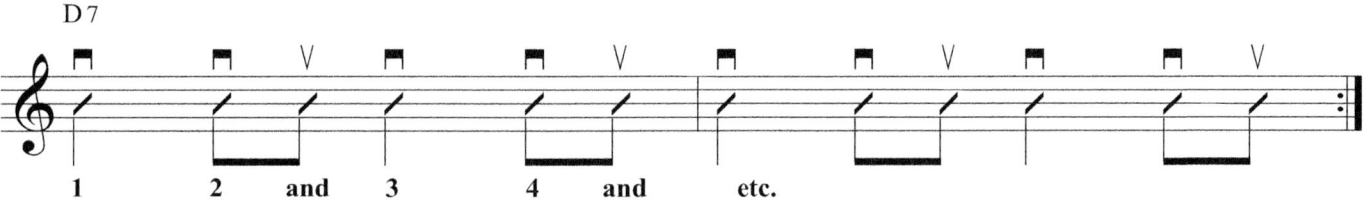

The next song follows the same form as "Sunshine," but also uses the new eighth note rhythms and repeat signs.

Spring Time

Lesson 8: A Major & E7

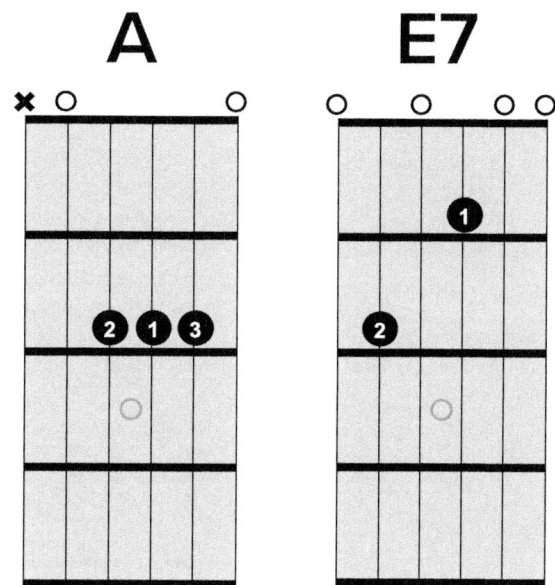

Try it: Practice the A major and E7 chords using the rhythms below.

Rhythm 1:

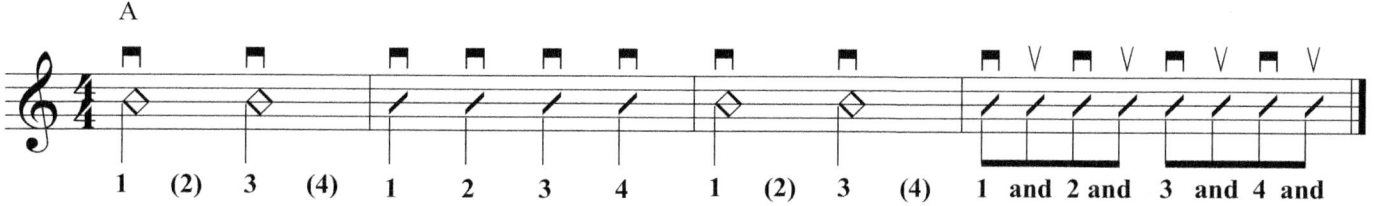

Rhythm 2:

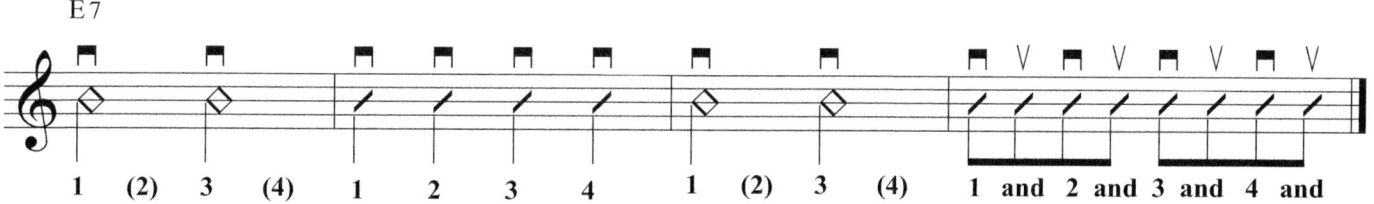

Rhythm 3:

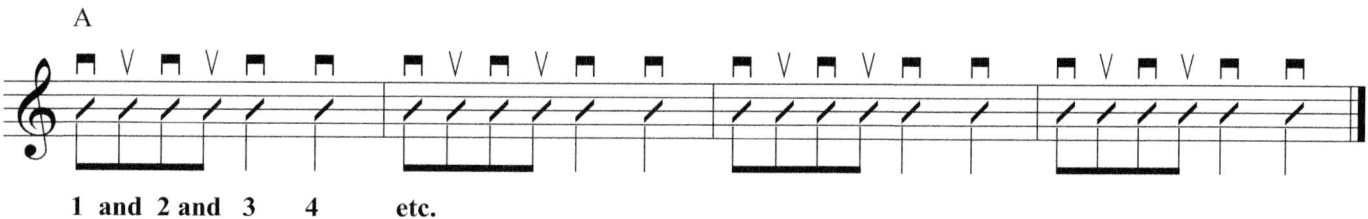

Practicing A Major and E7

Exercise 1:

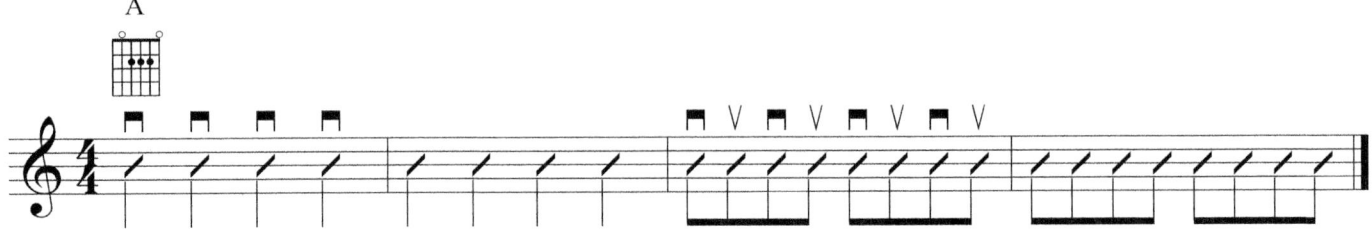

Exercise 2:

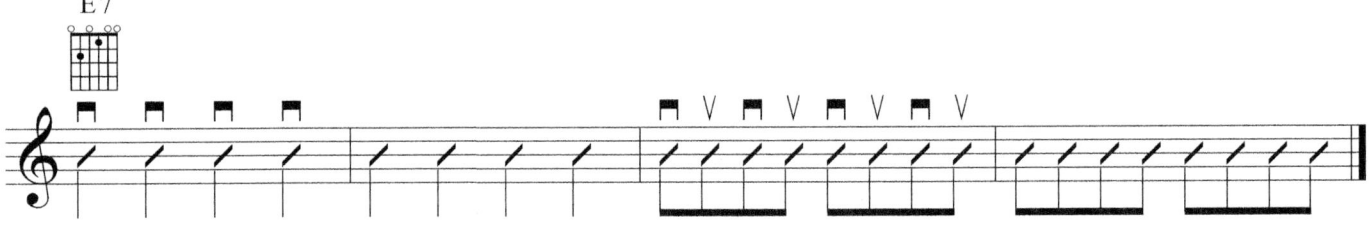

Exercise 3:

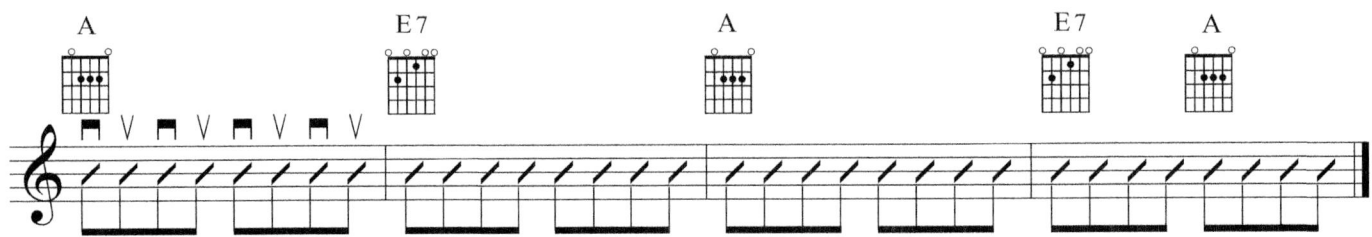

Exercise 4:

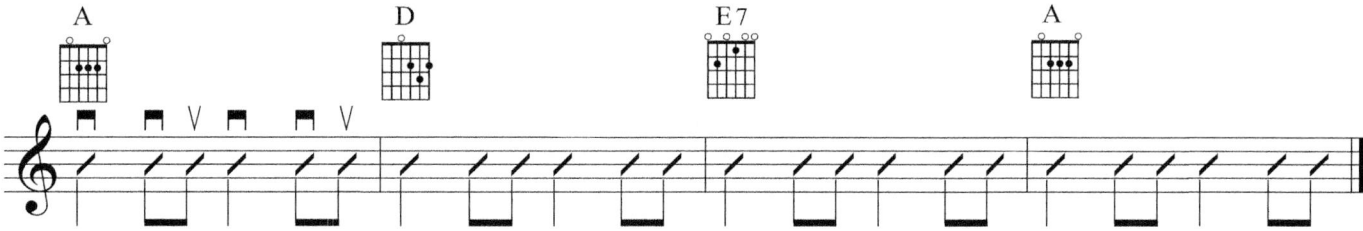

Exercise 5:

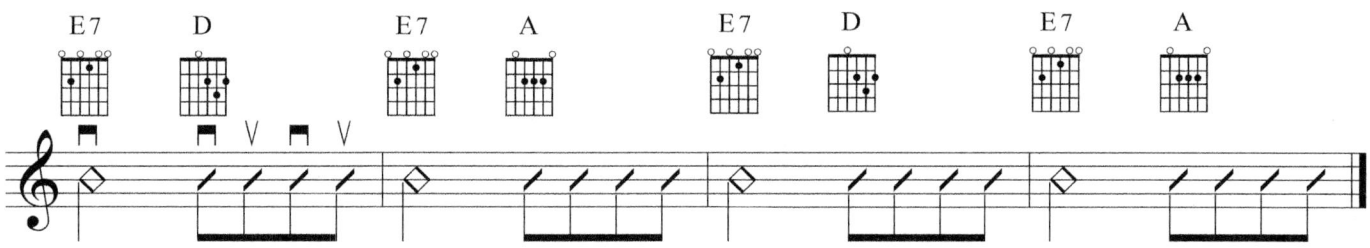

Exercise 6:

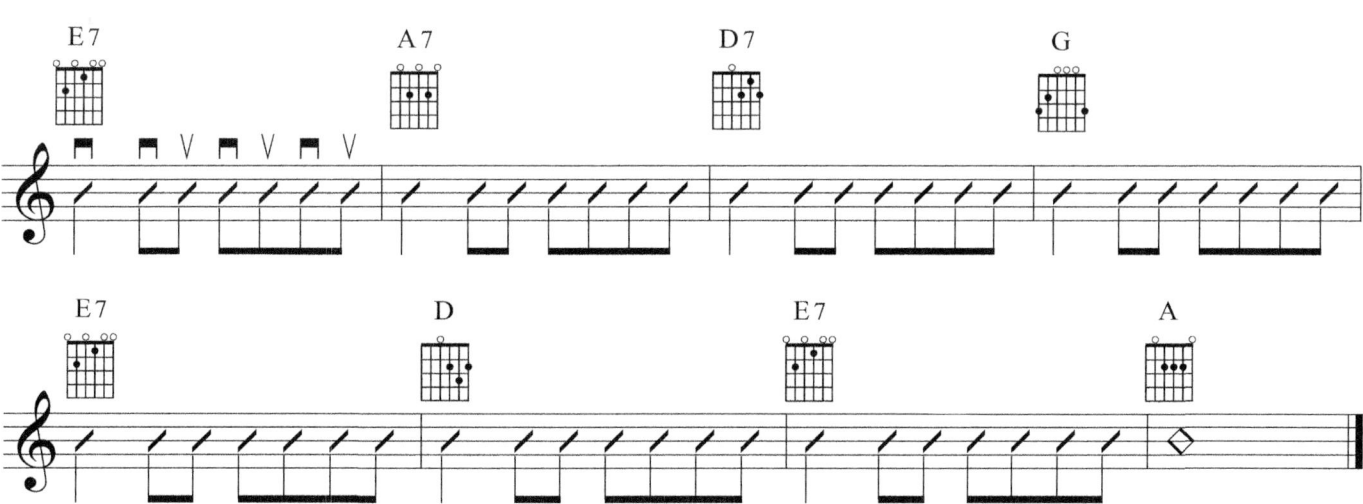

This next song includes a bridge. A **bridge** is a section of music that allows the listener a moment of reflection. It is often different from either the verse or chorus in some way.

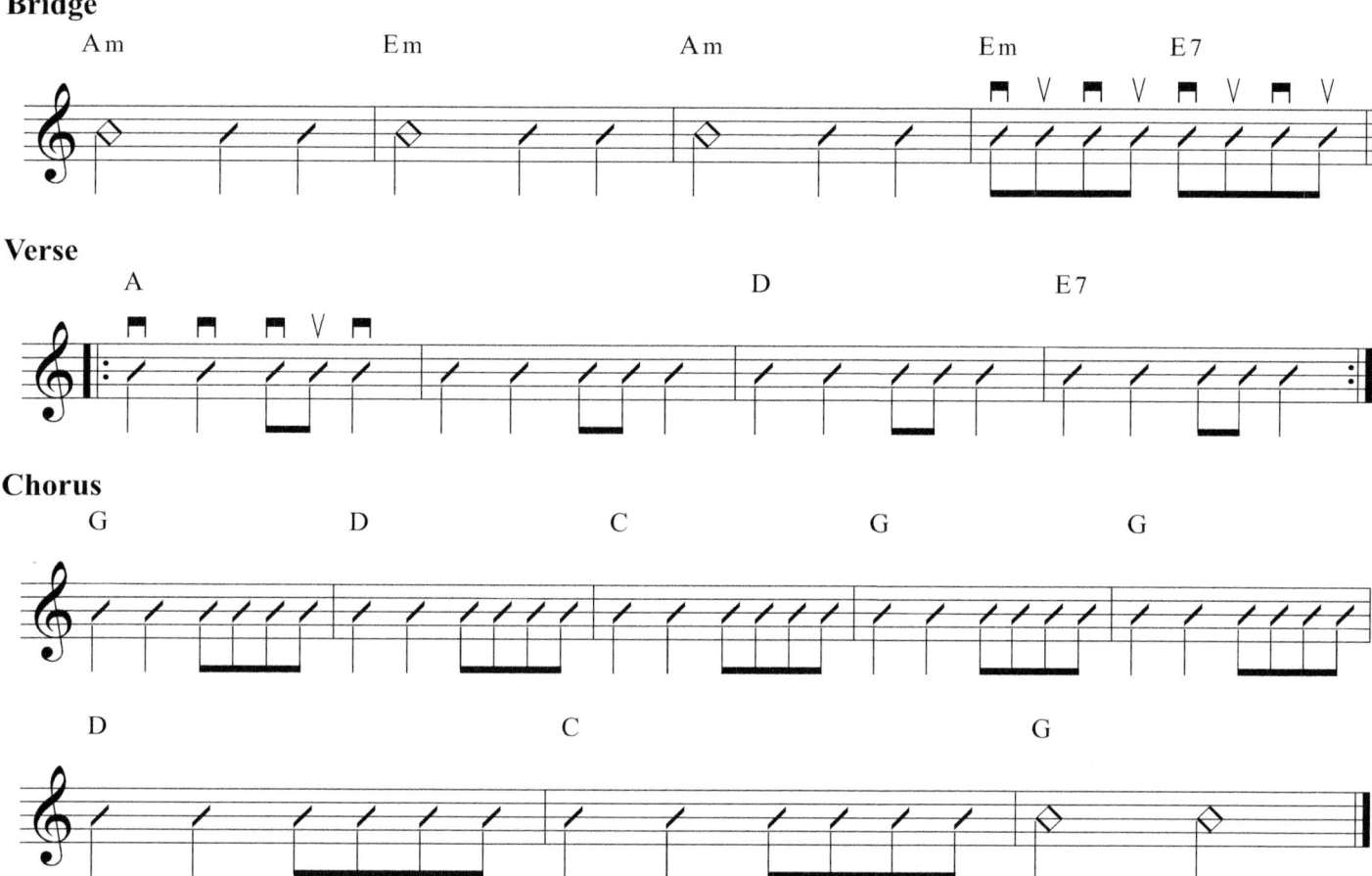

Lesson 9: E Major & B7

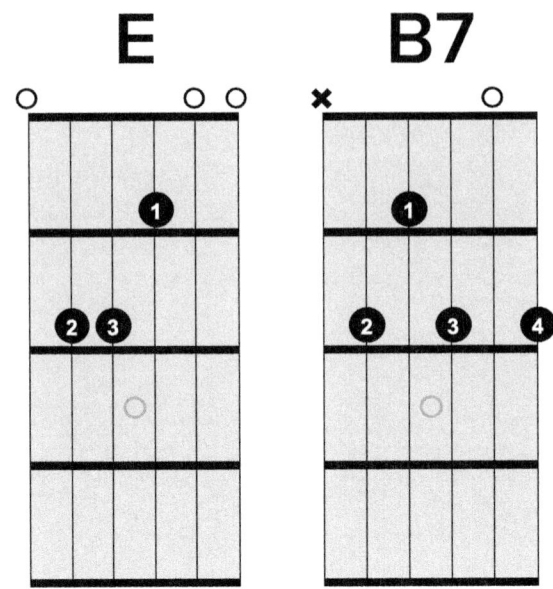

Try it: Practice the E major and B7 chords using the rhythms below.

Rhythm 1:

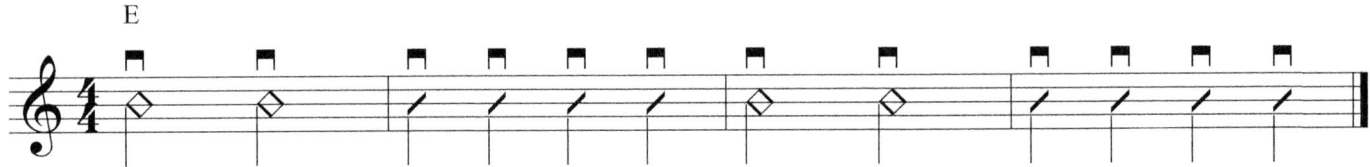

Rhythm 2:

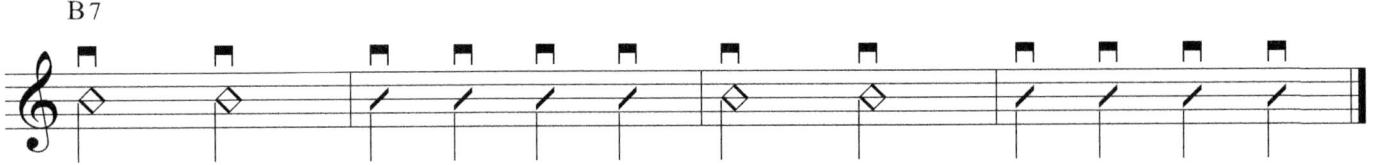

Rhythm 3:

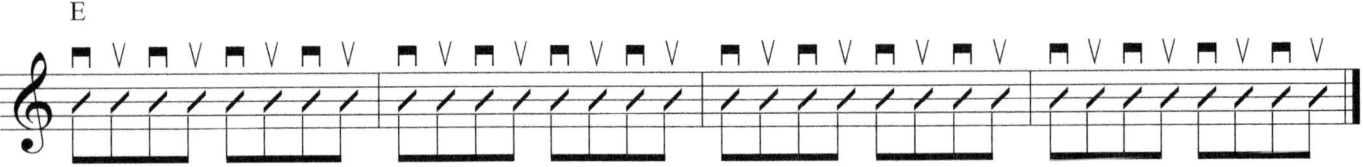

Practicing E Major and B7

Exercise 1:

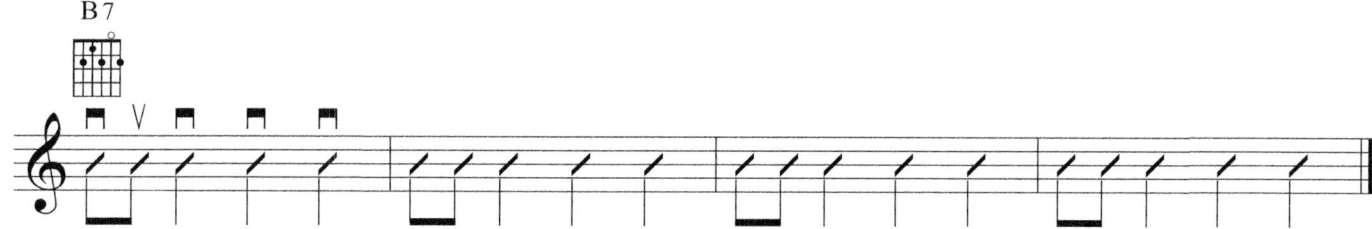

Exercise 2:

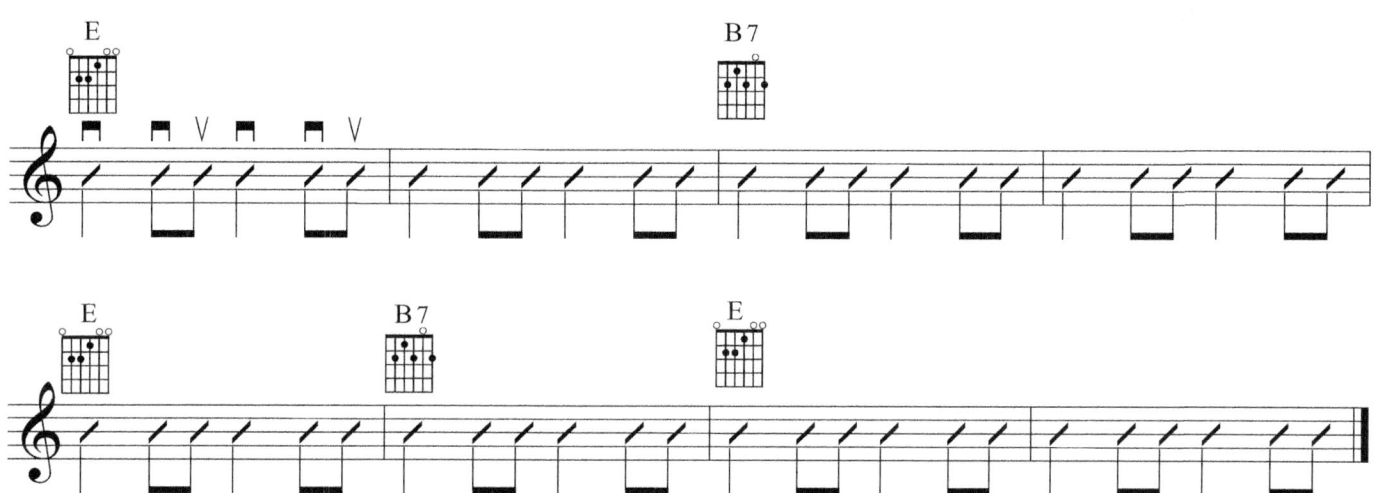

Exercise 3:

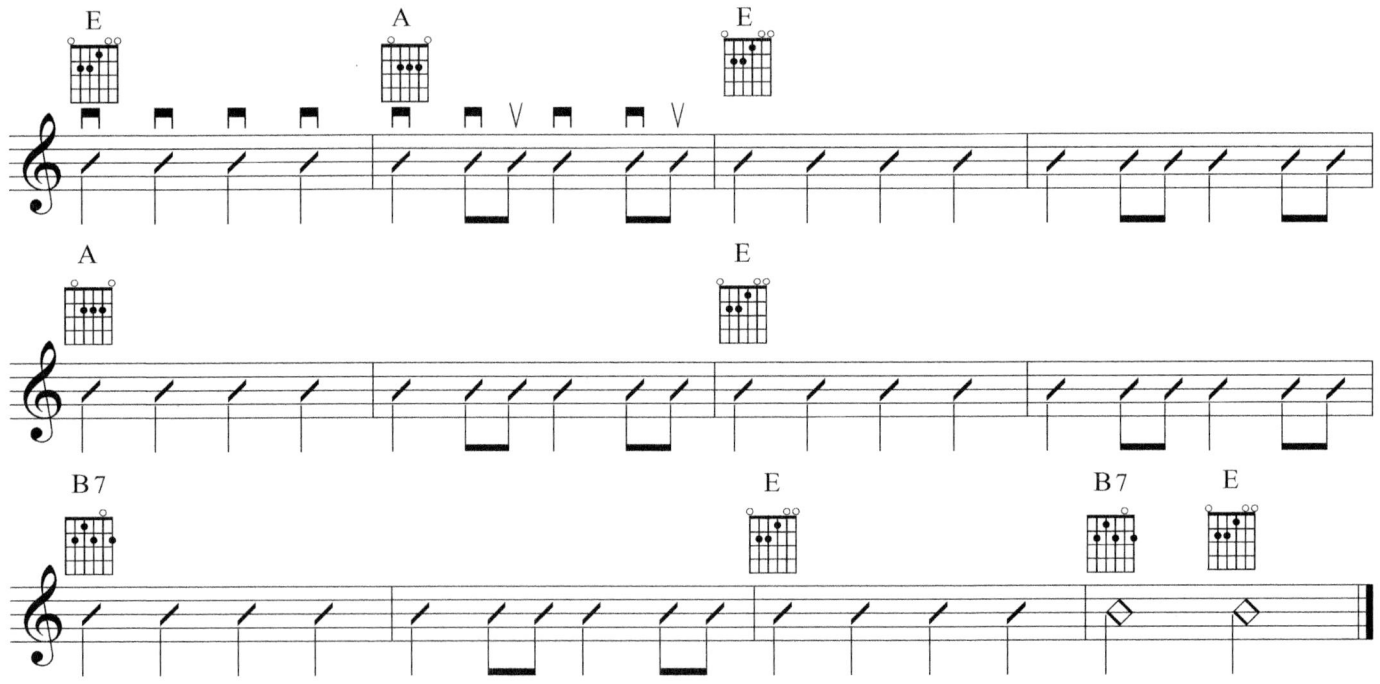

Review:
G, Em, C, Am, D, A7, A, E7, E, & B7

Chord Progression 1

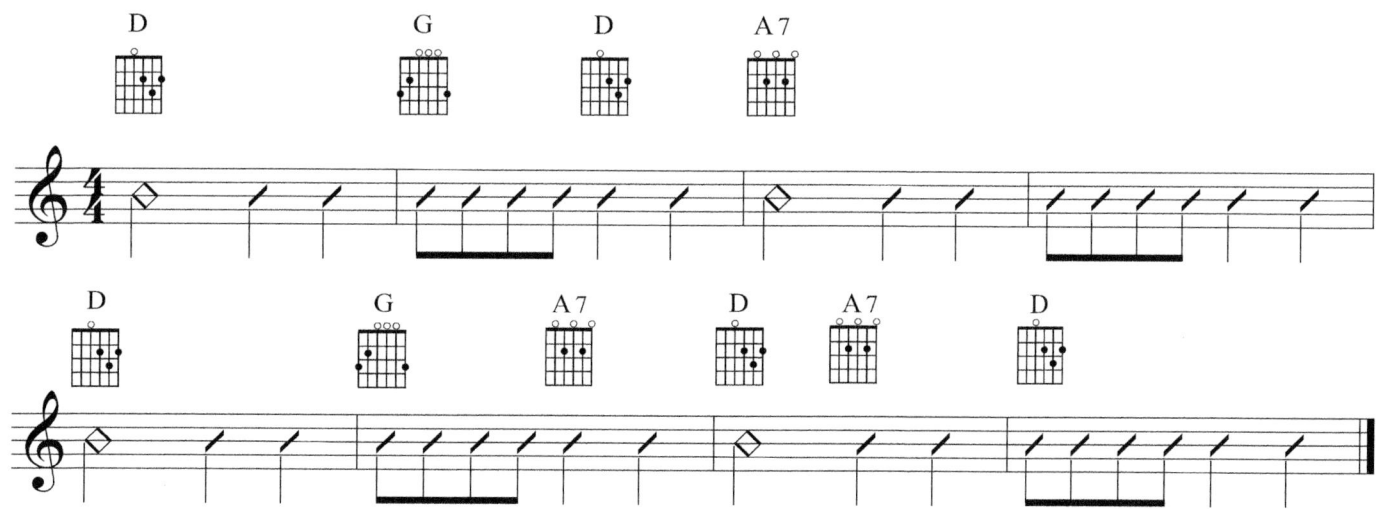

Chord Progression 2

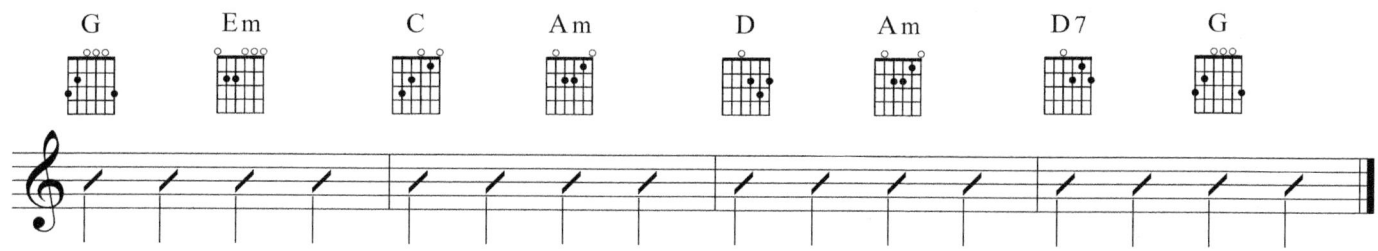

Chord Progression 3

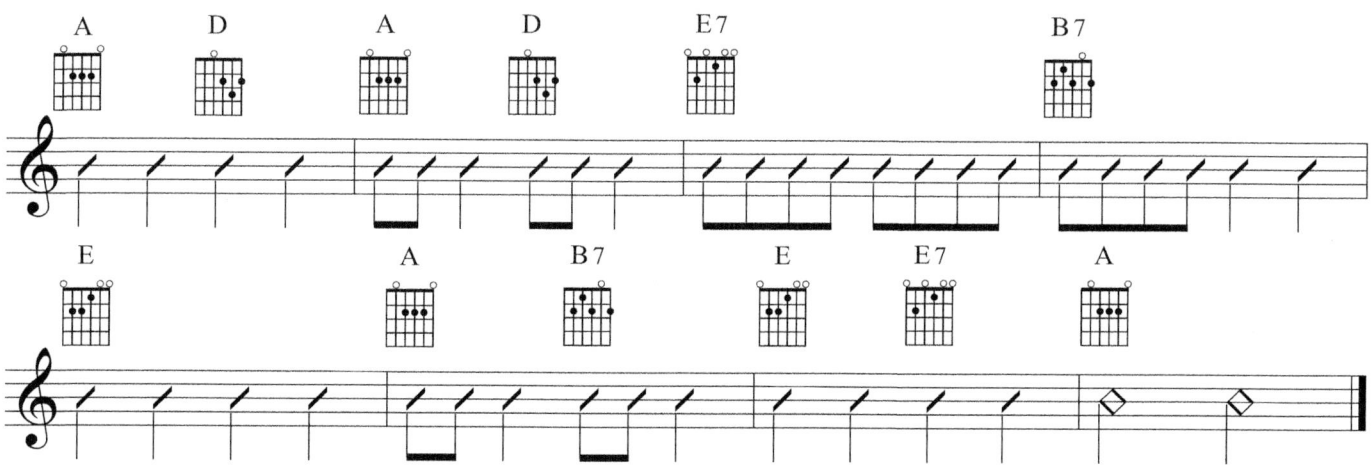

Chord Progression 4

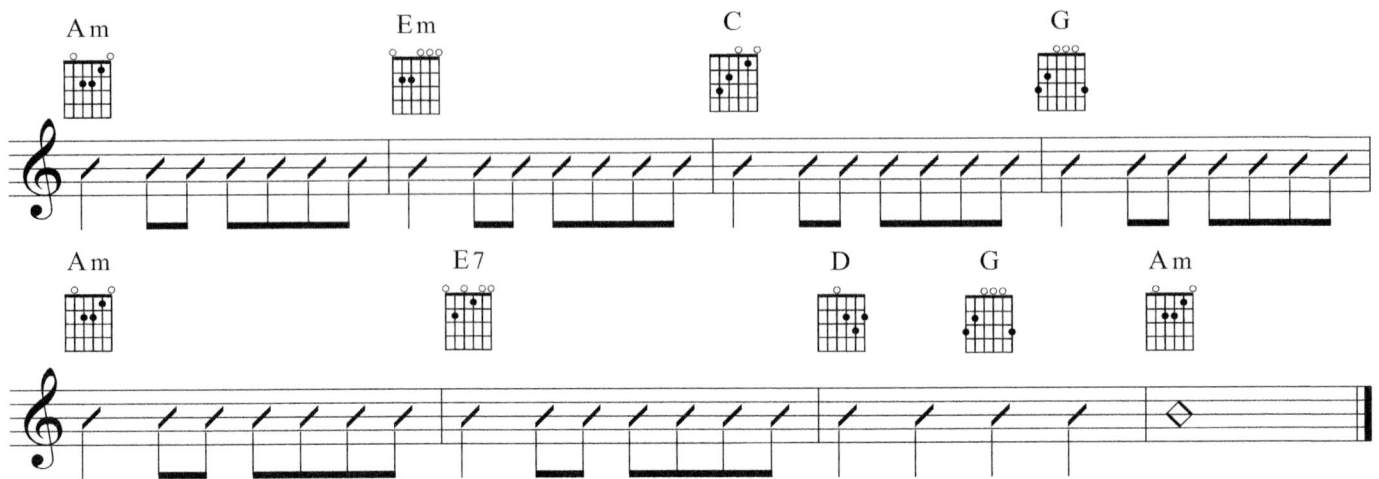

Chord Progression 5

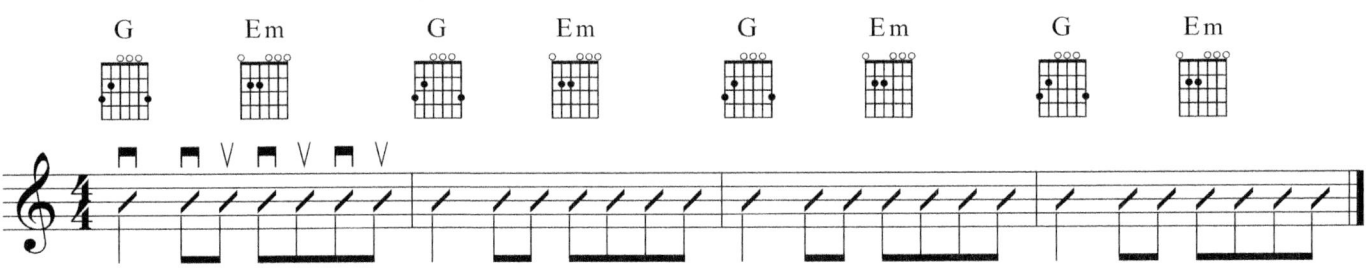

Chord Progression 6

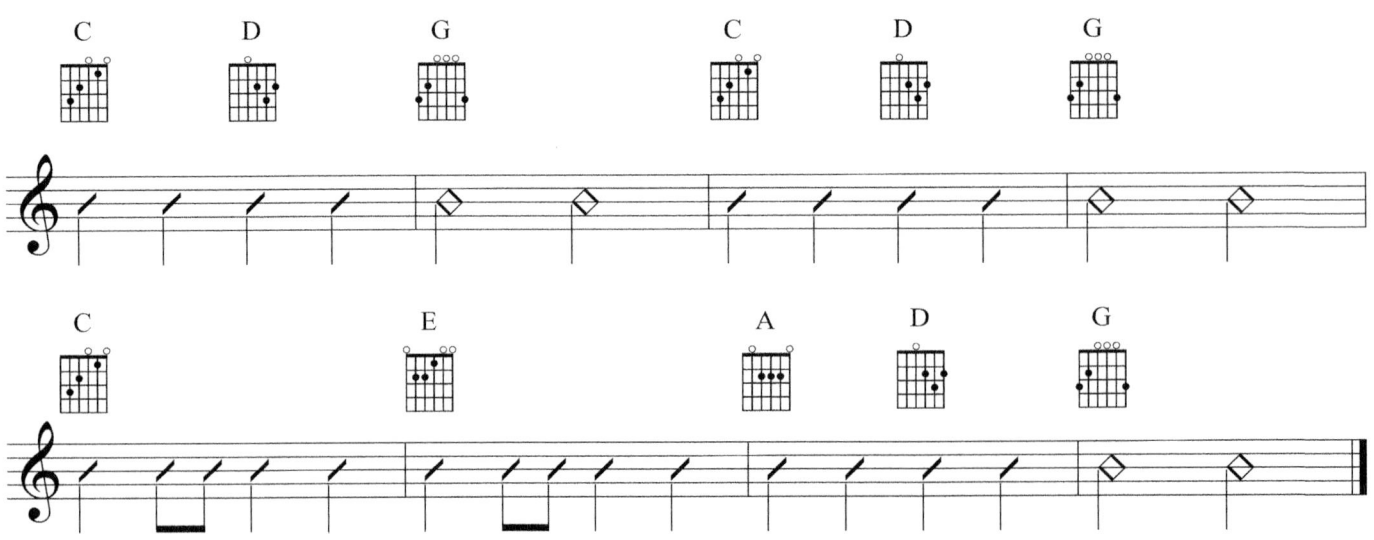

Chord Progression 7

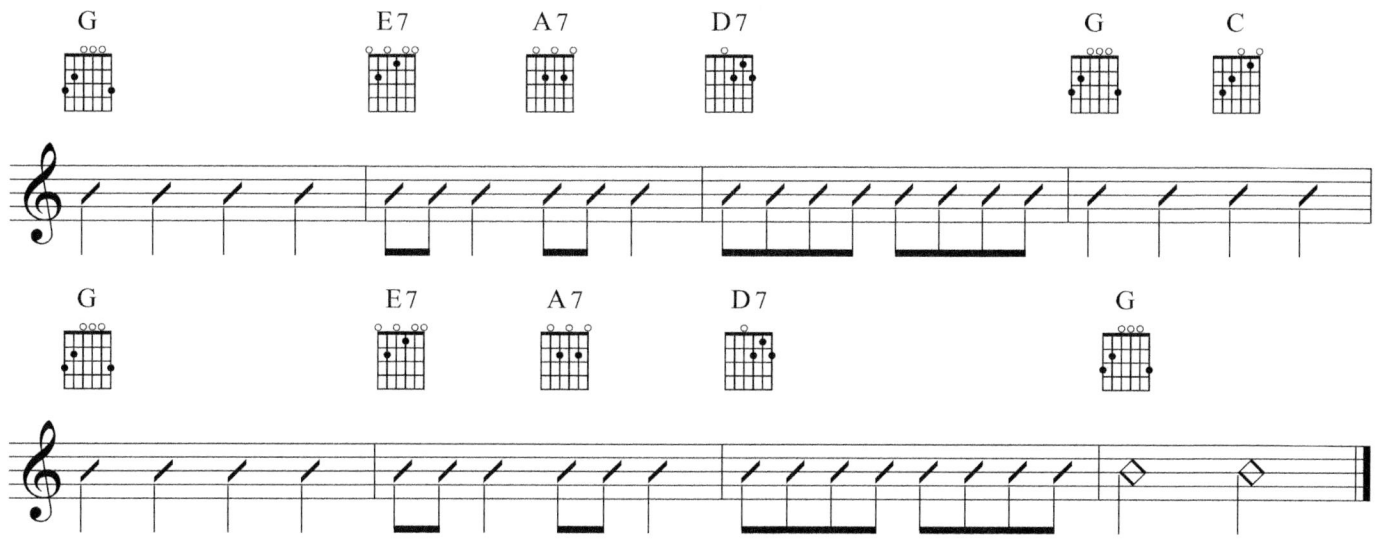

Chord Progression 8

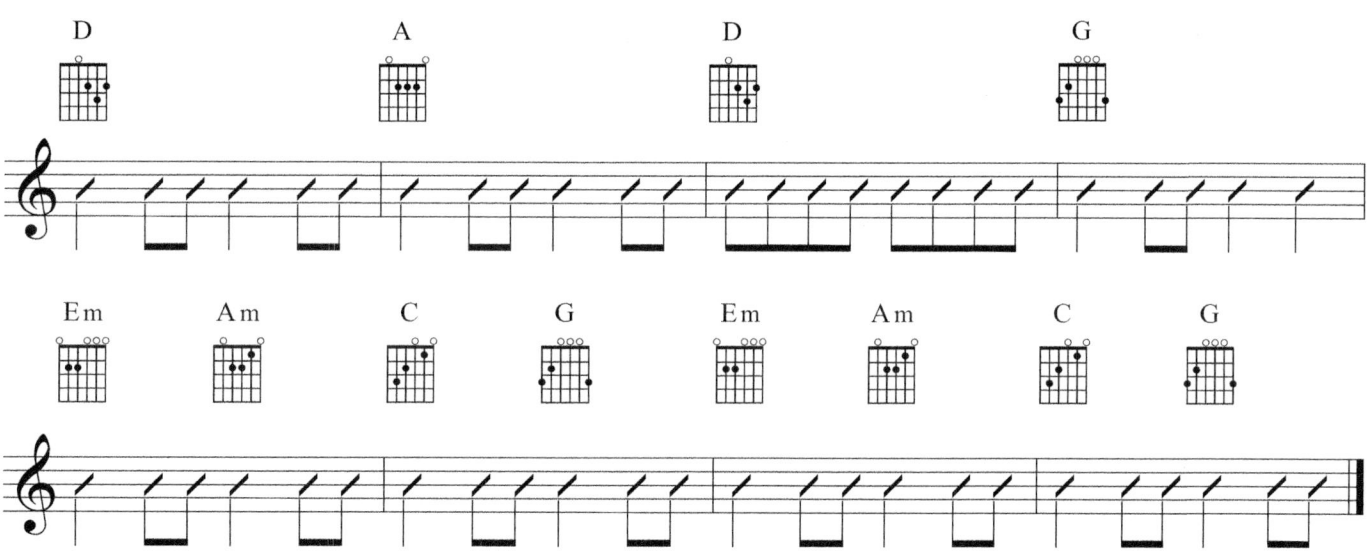

Lesson 10: D Minor

Dm

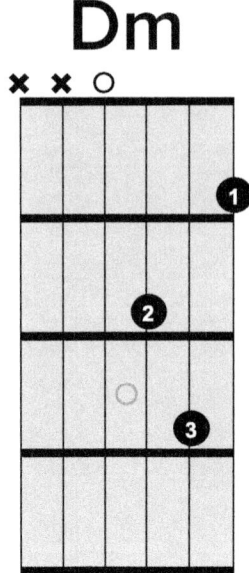

Try it: Practice the D minor chord below using the suggested rhythms. Note that you only strum four strings on this chord.

Rhythm 1:

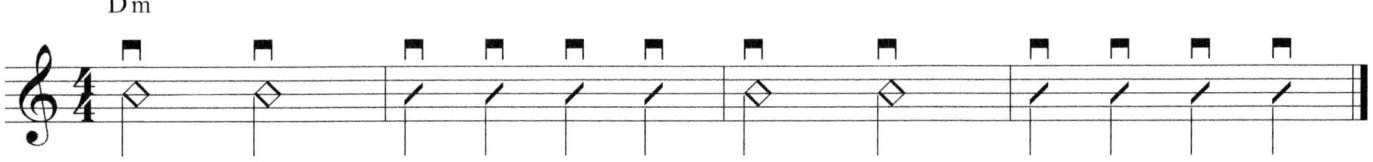

Rhythm 2:

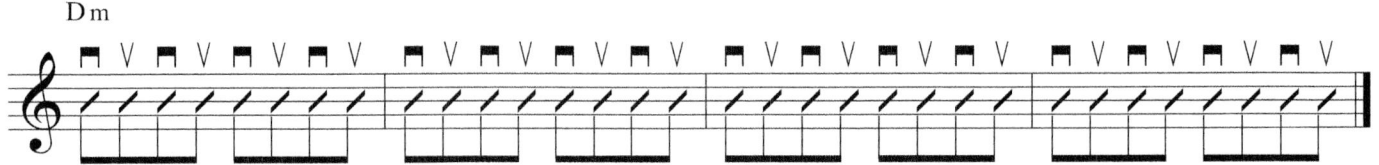

Rhythm 3:

Practicing Dm

Exercise 1: Moving between Dm and Am

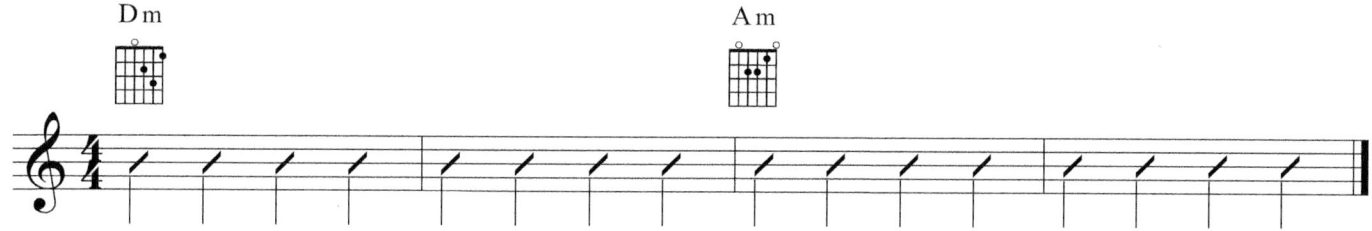

Exercise 2: Dm and Am with eighth notes

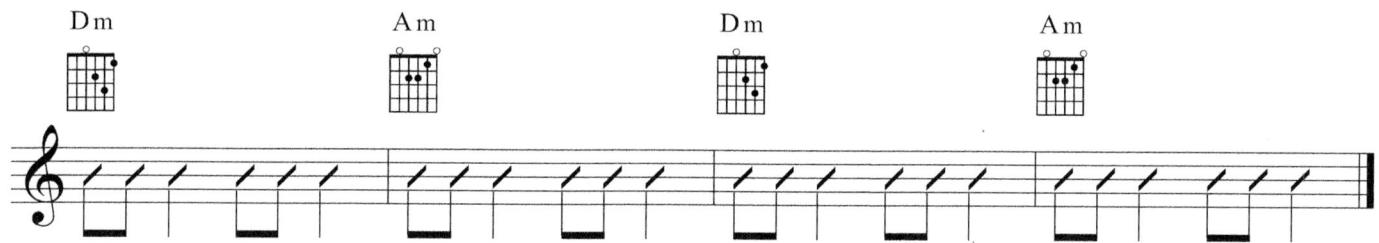

Exercise 3: Moving among Dm, C, and G

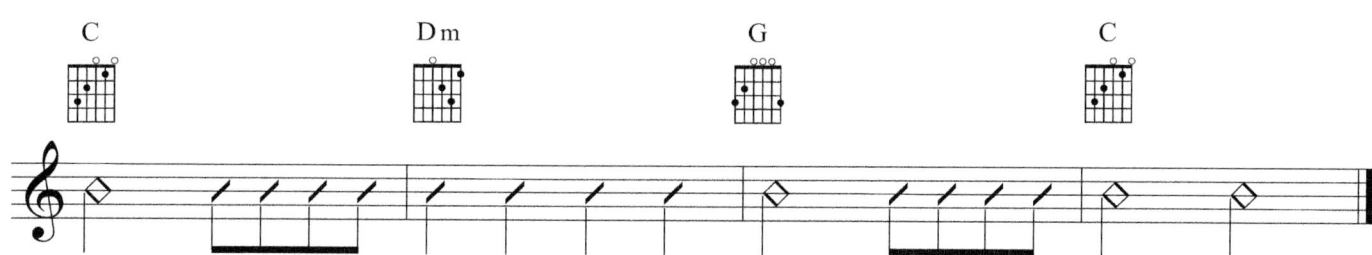

Exercise 4: Moving among Dm, Am, Em, and E7

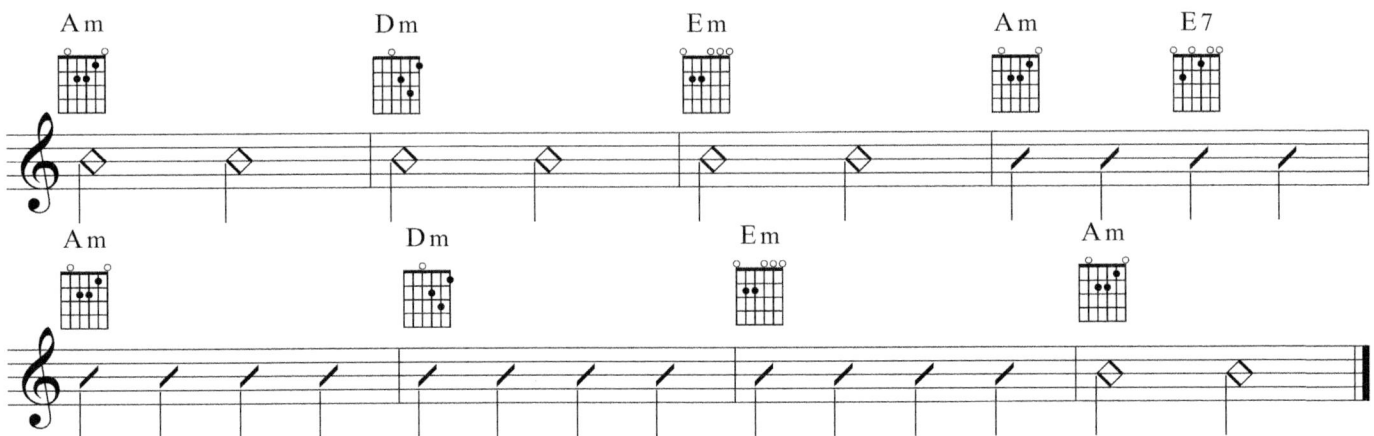

Exercise 5: Moving among Dm, A7, and G

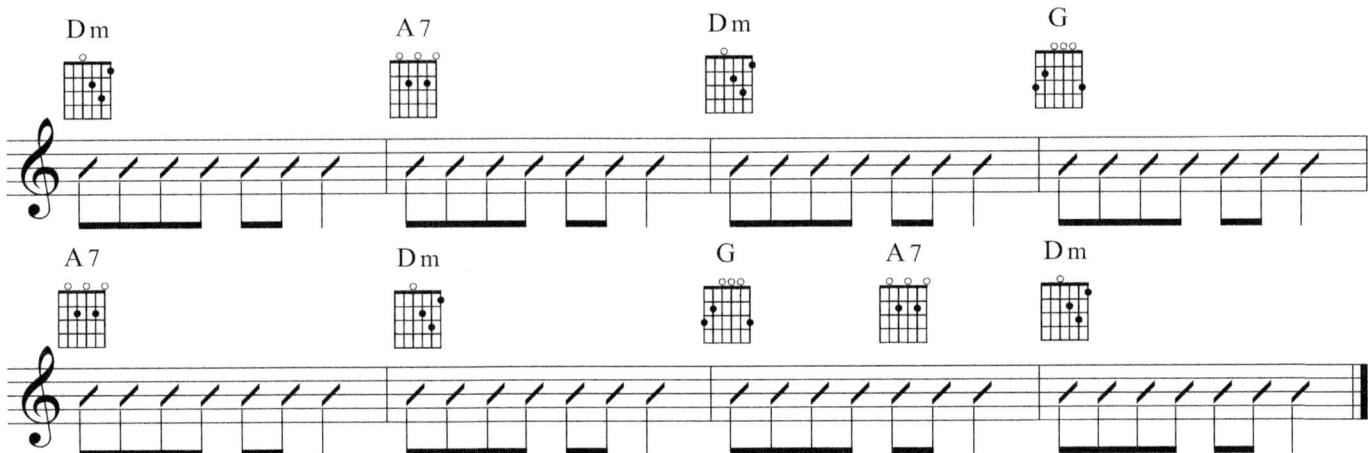

The following song includes an **introduction**. Most songs have an attention-getting intro that serves to set the mood and tone for the song. Oftentimes, the bridge and introduction are the same, but not always.

Riding Home

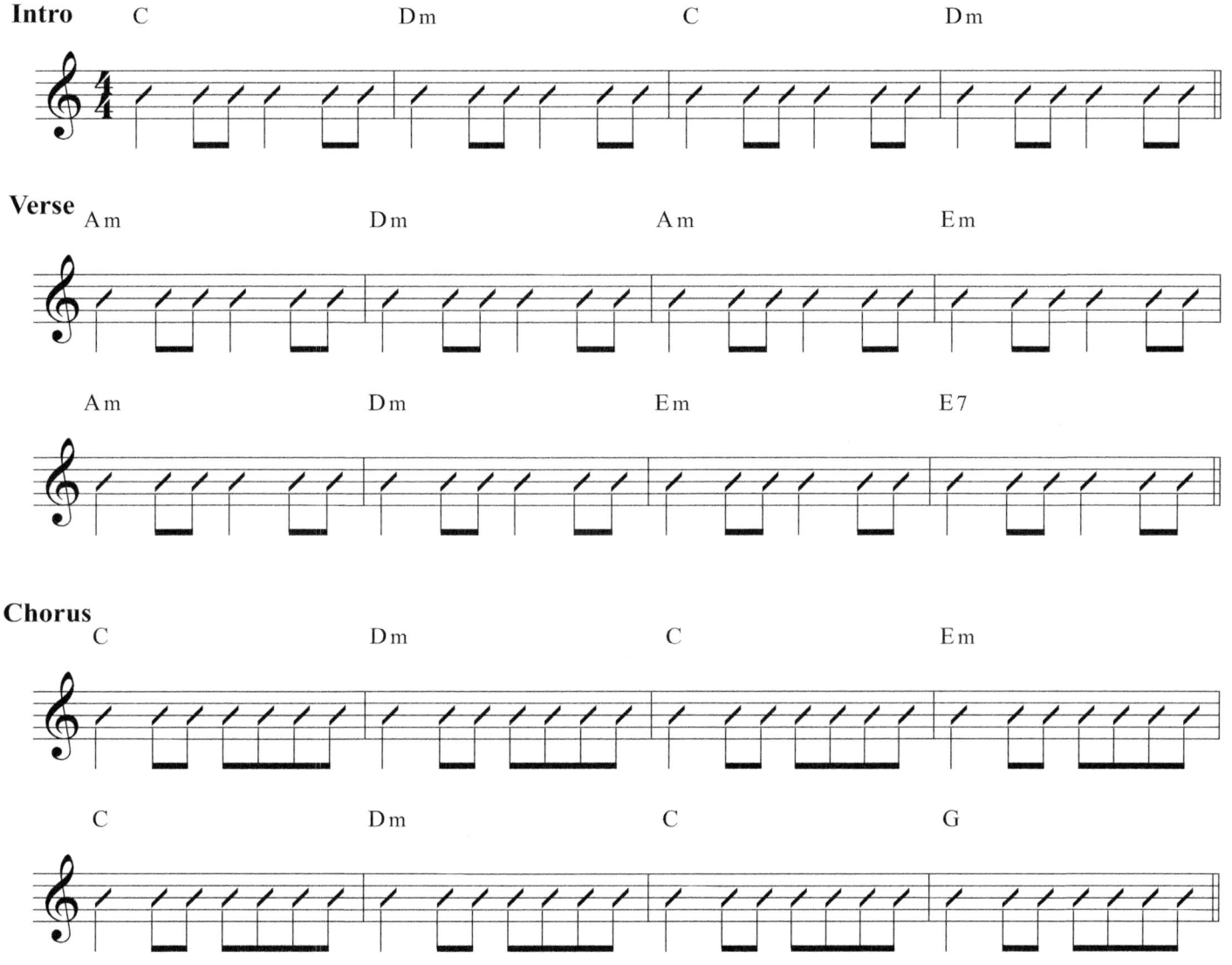

(Note that the song continues on the following page)

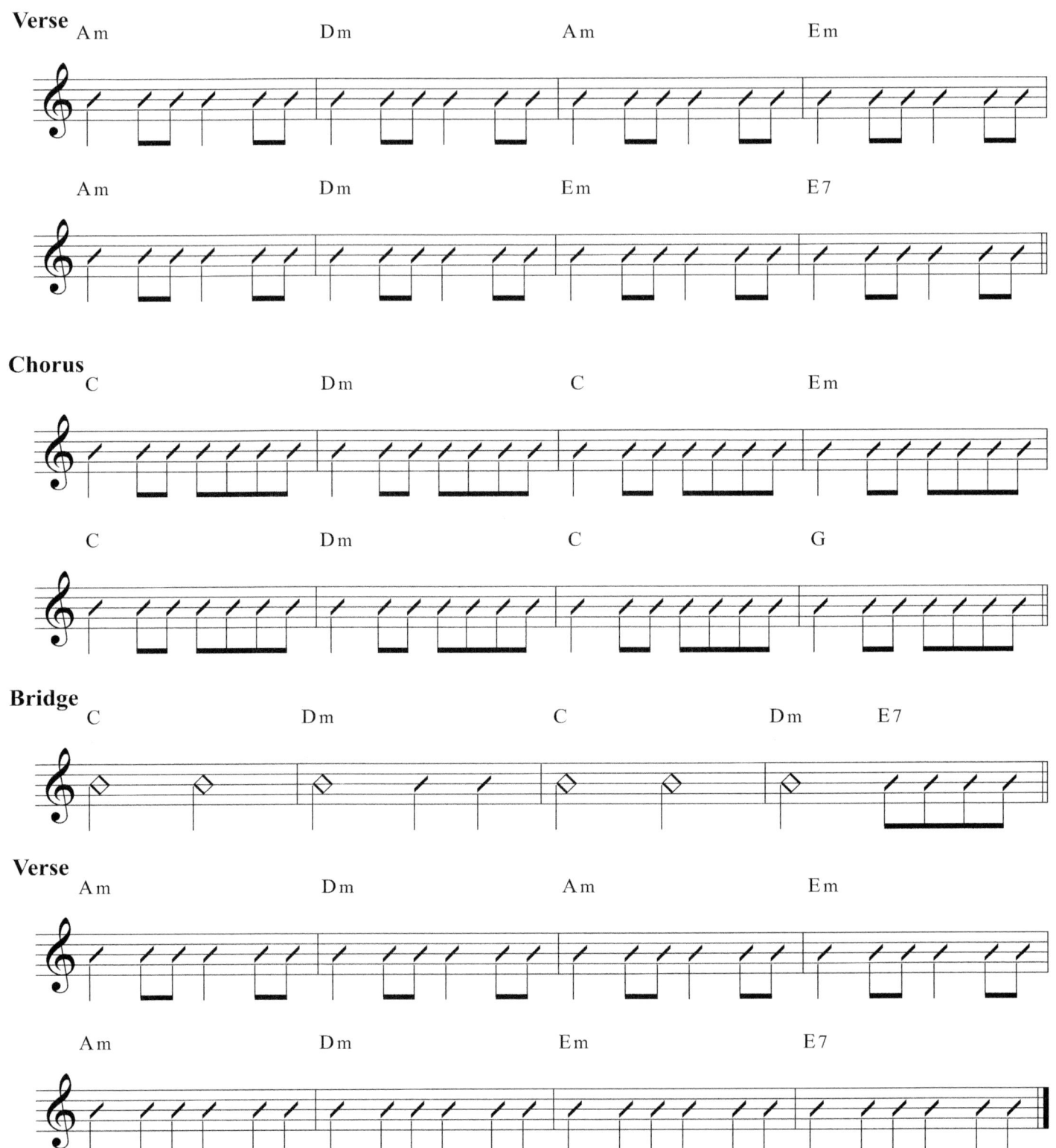

Lesson 11:
G7

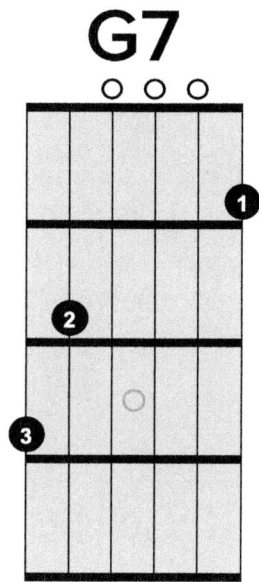

Try it: Practice the G7 chord using the rhythms below.

Rhythm 1:

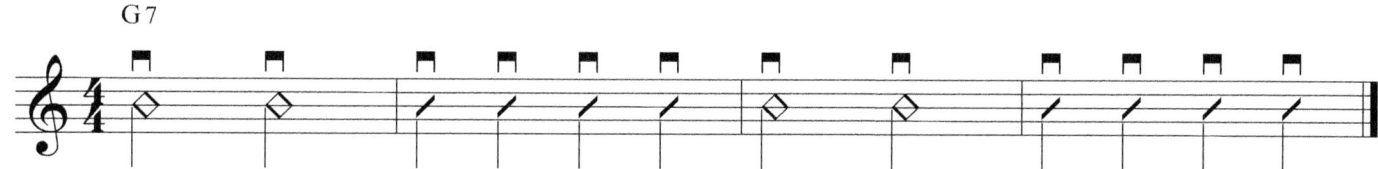

Rhythm 2:

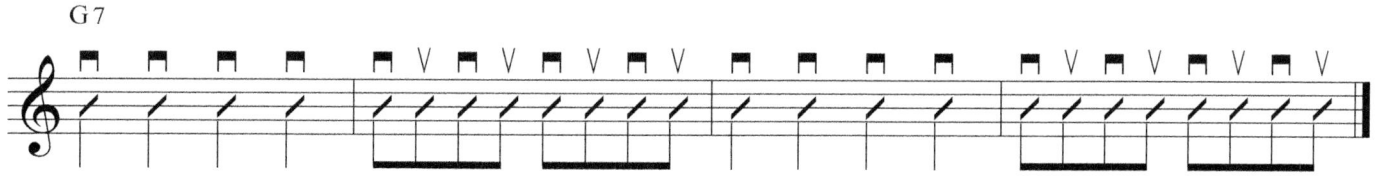

Rhythm 3:

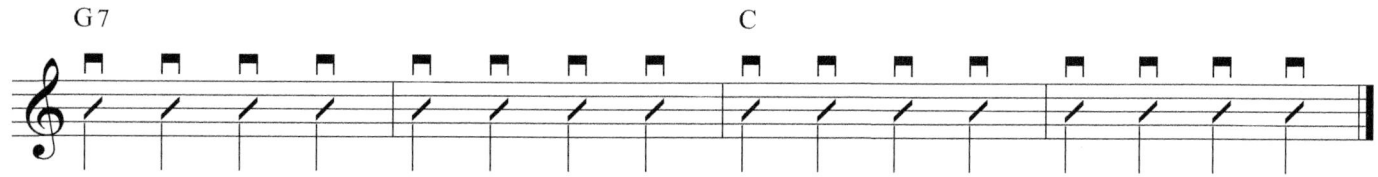

Practicing G7

Exercise 1: Moving between G7 and C

> **Tip:**
> Notice how each chord uses the same fingers and same basic shape, but on different sets of strings.

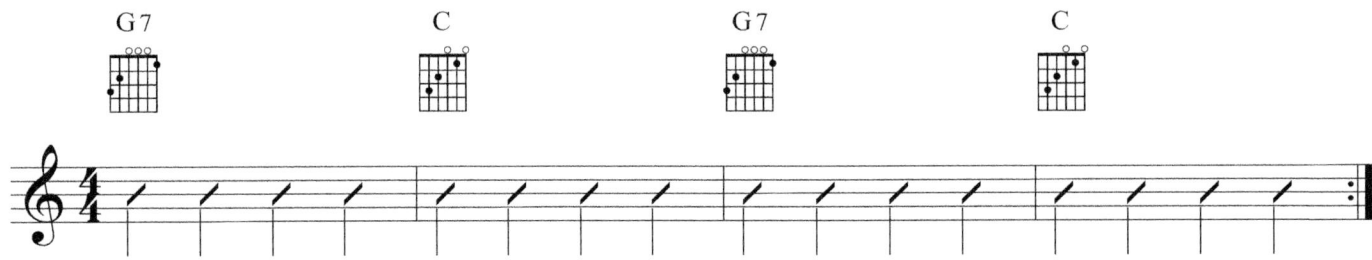

Exercise 2: Moving between G7, C, and Am

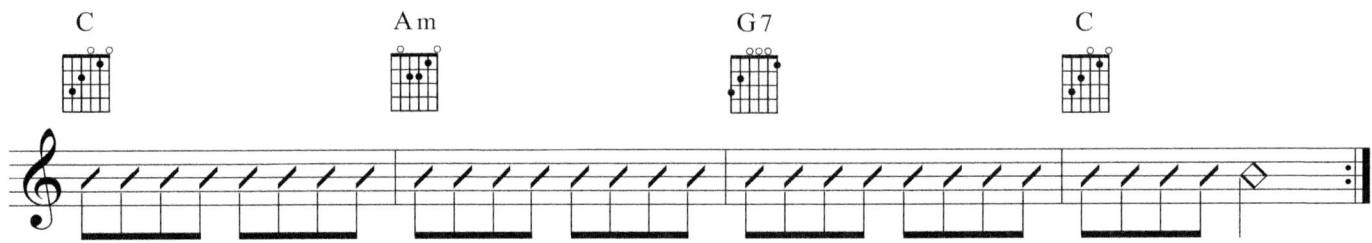

Exercise 3:

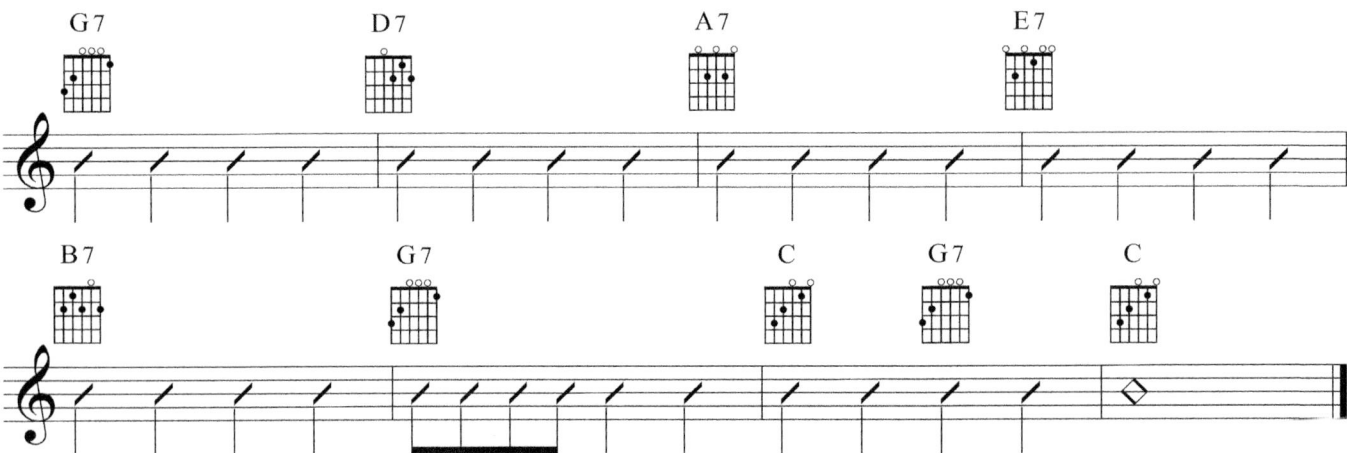

Exercise 4:

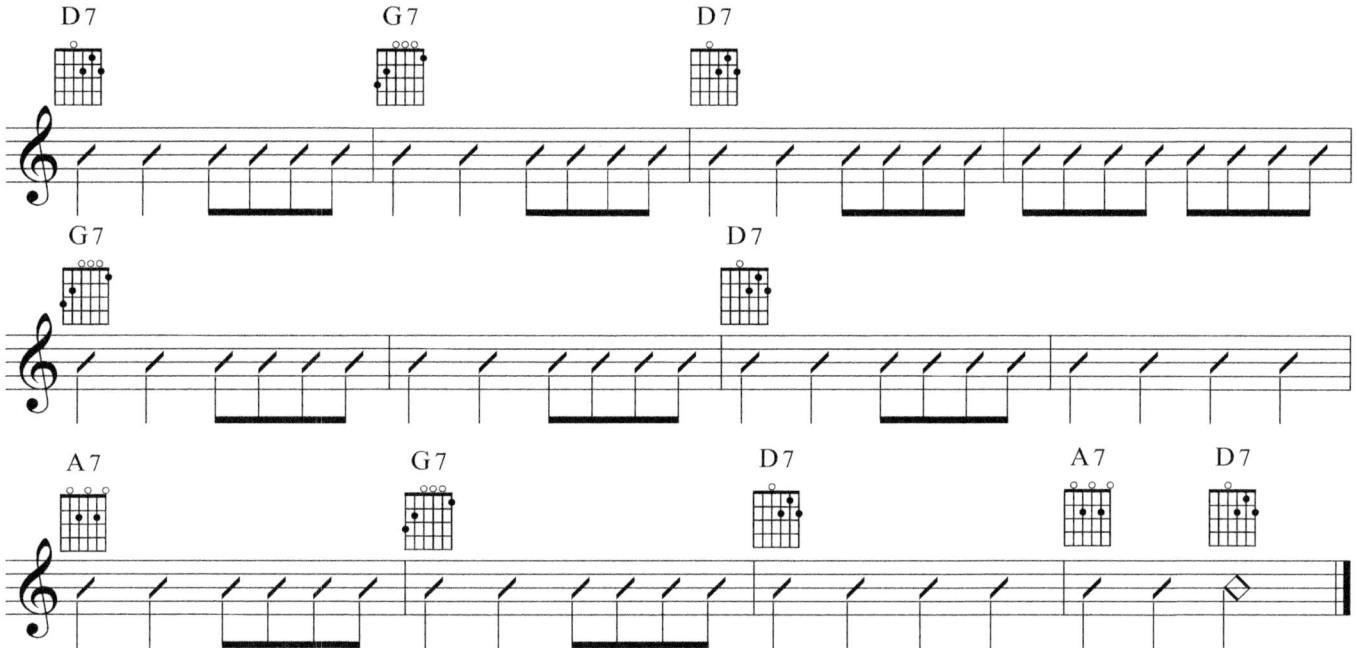

The example song on the next page contains a new element called the **outro**, which is simply an ending section of the song. This song also contains all the elements from previous song examples: intro, verse, chorus, and bridge.

Friday Night

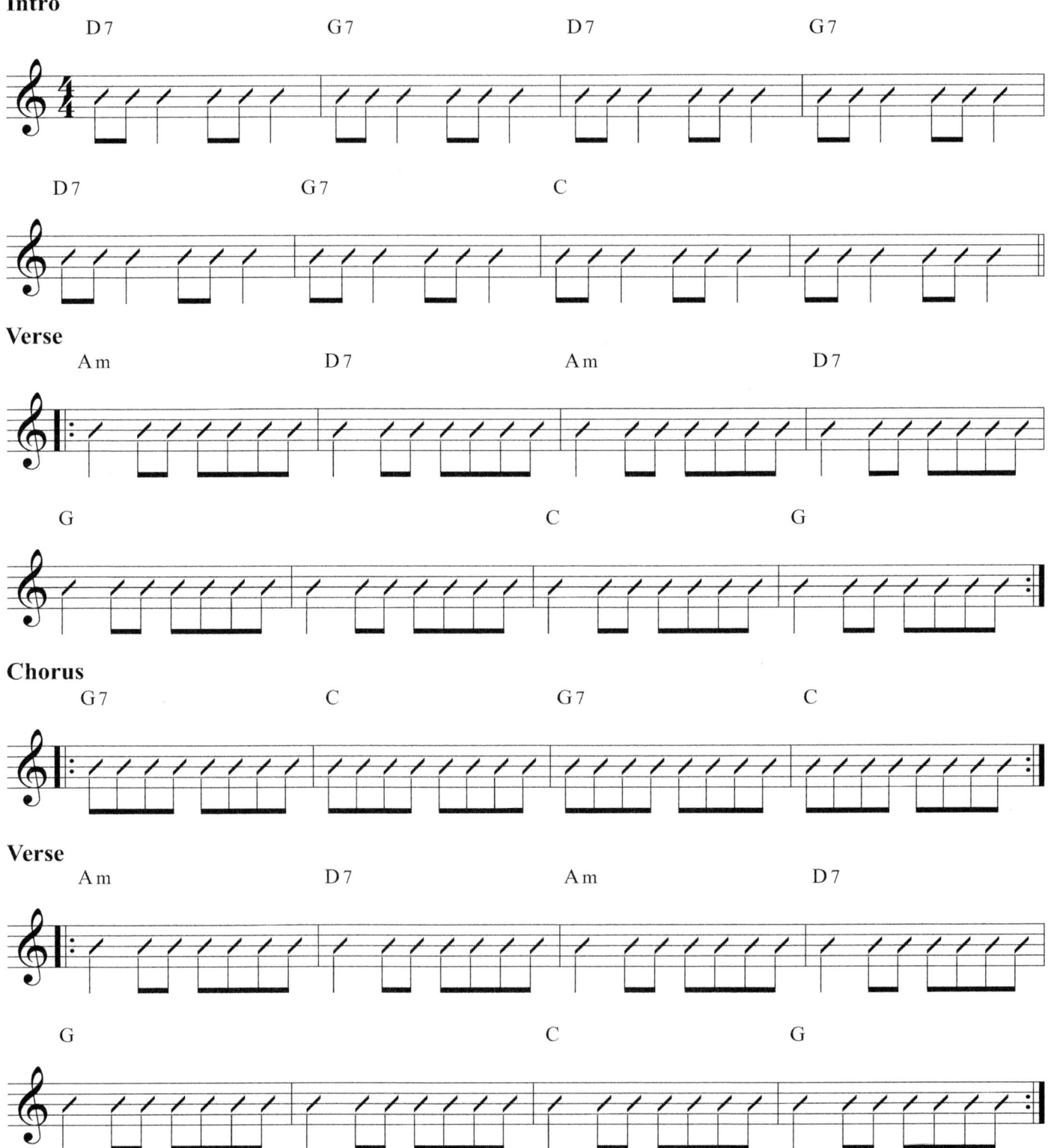

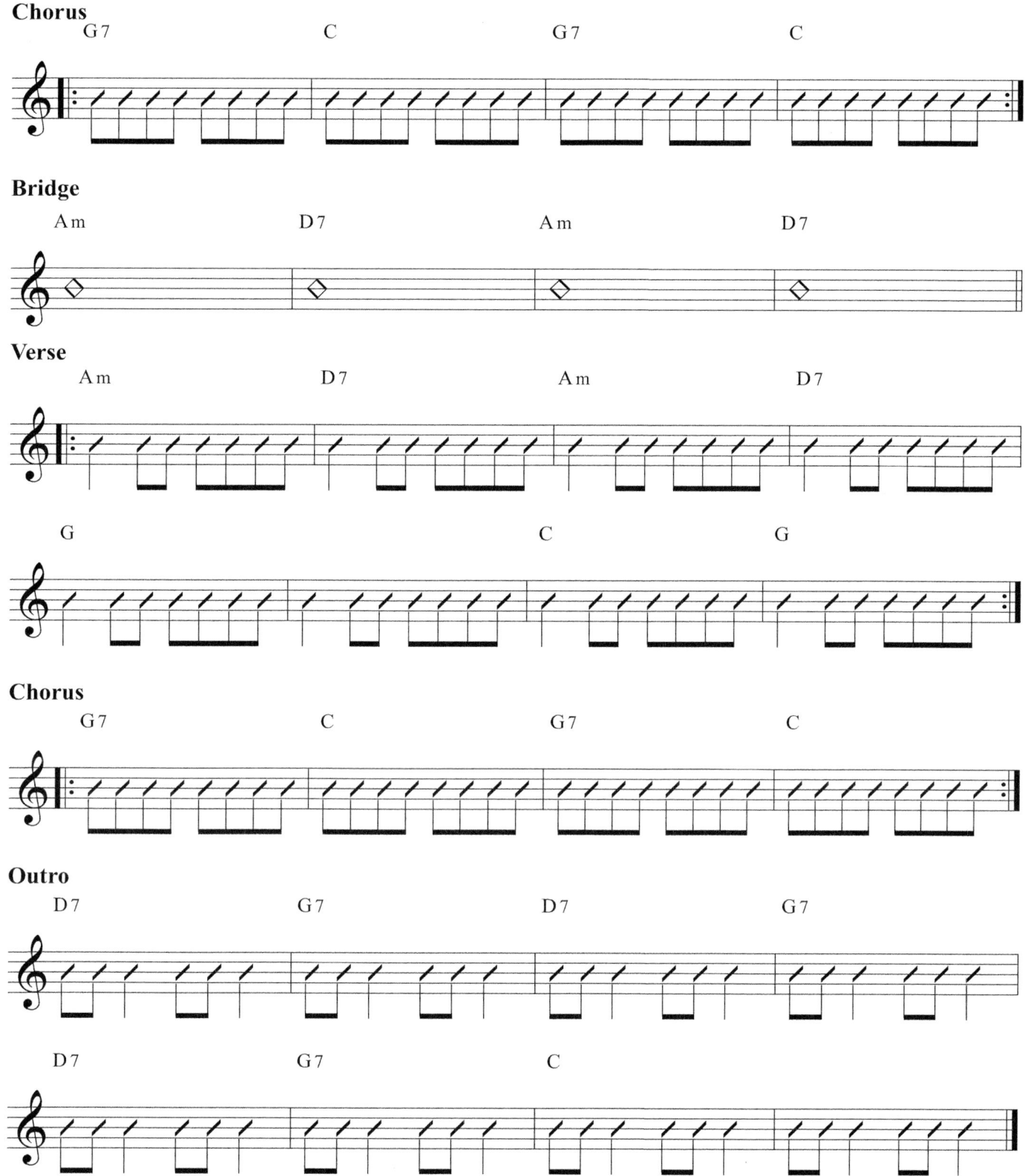

The next song includes a **pre chorus**. The pre chorus is used to set up the chorus. Not all songs include a pre chorus.

Diamond

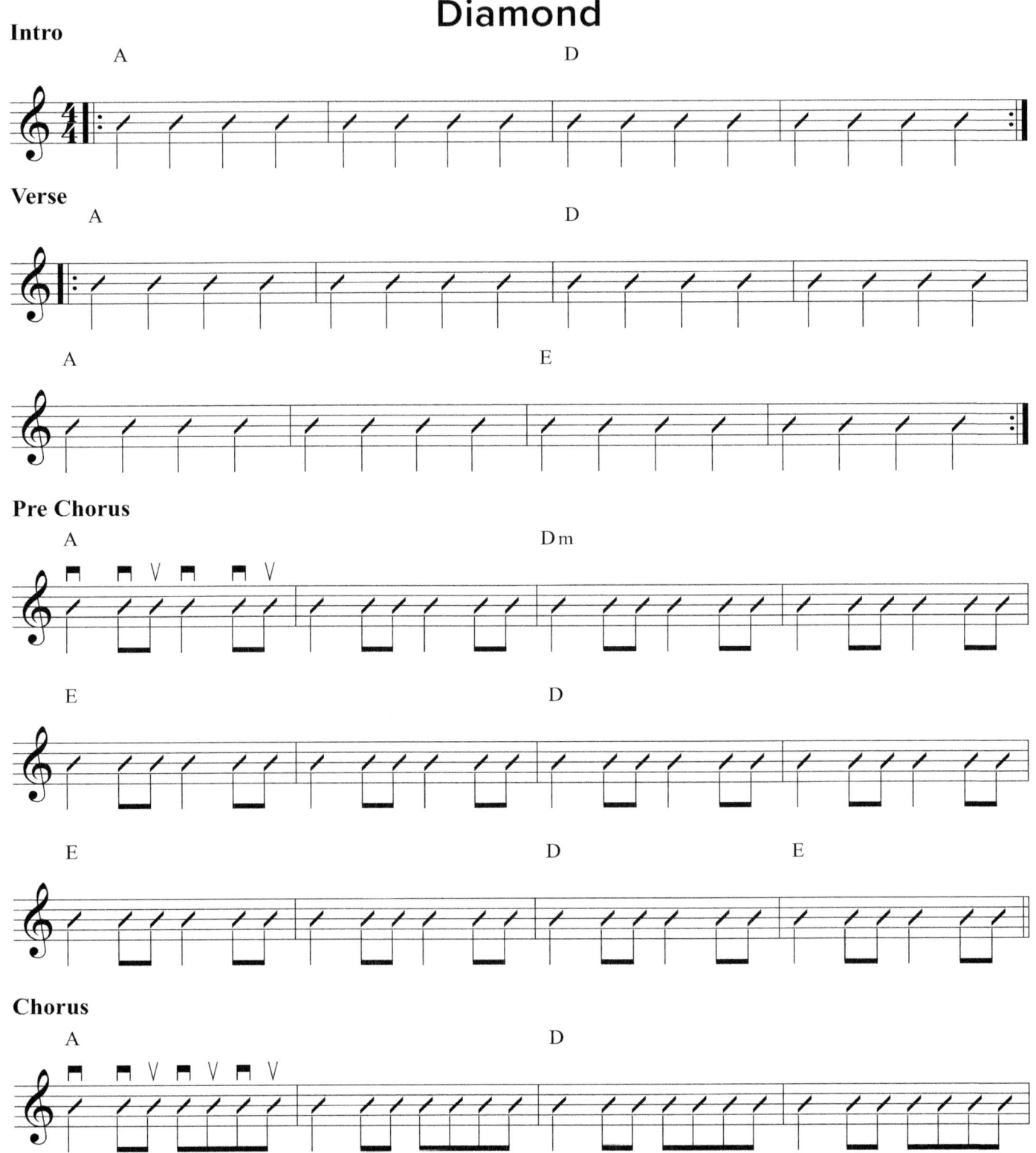

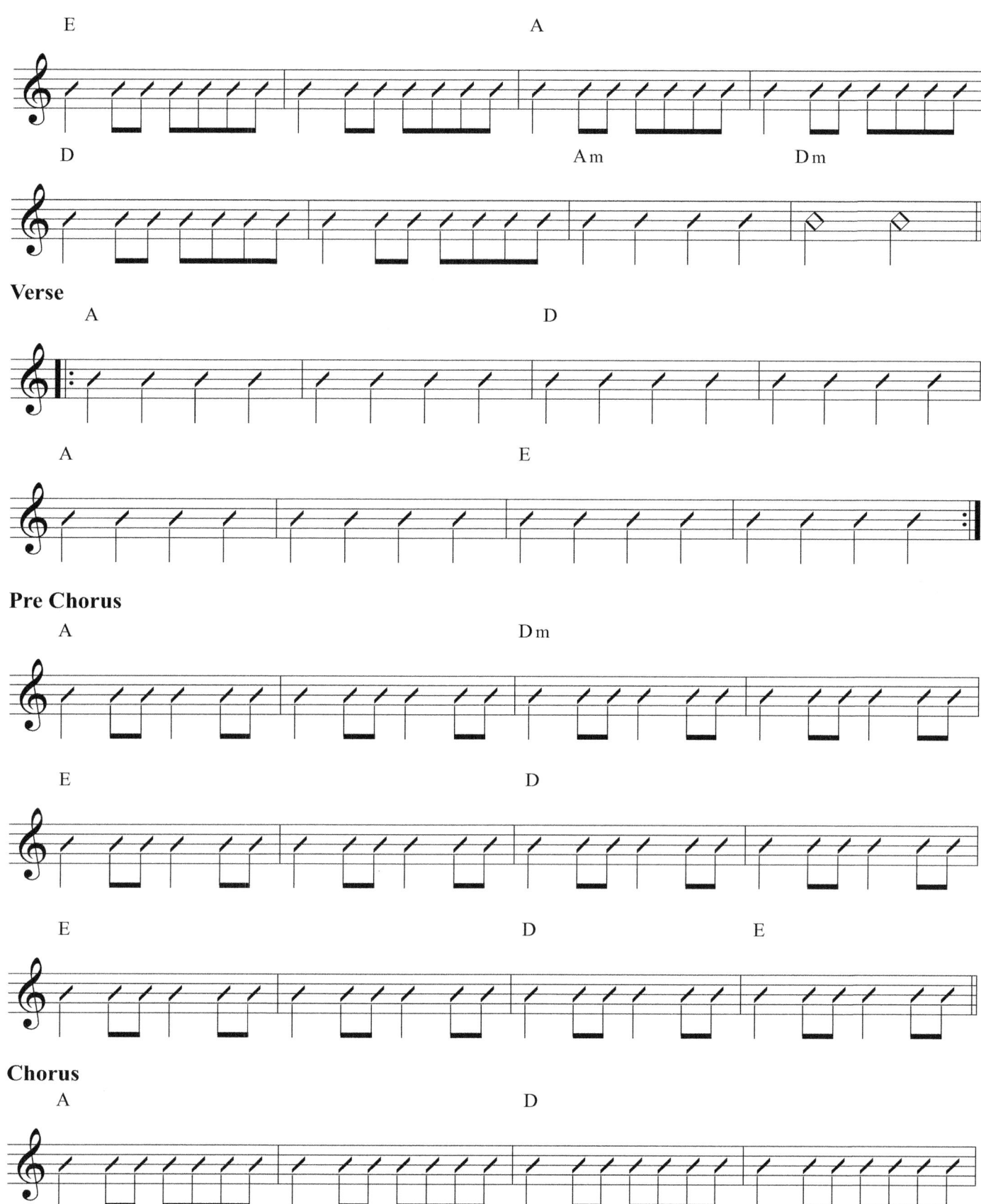

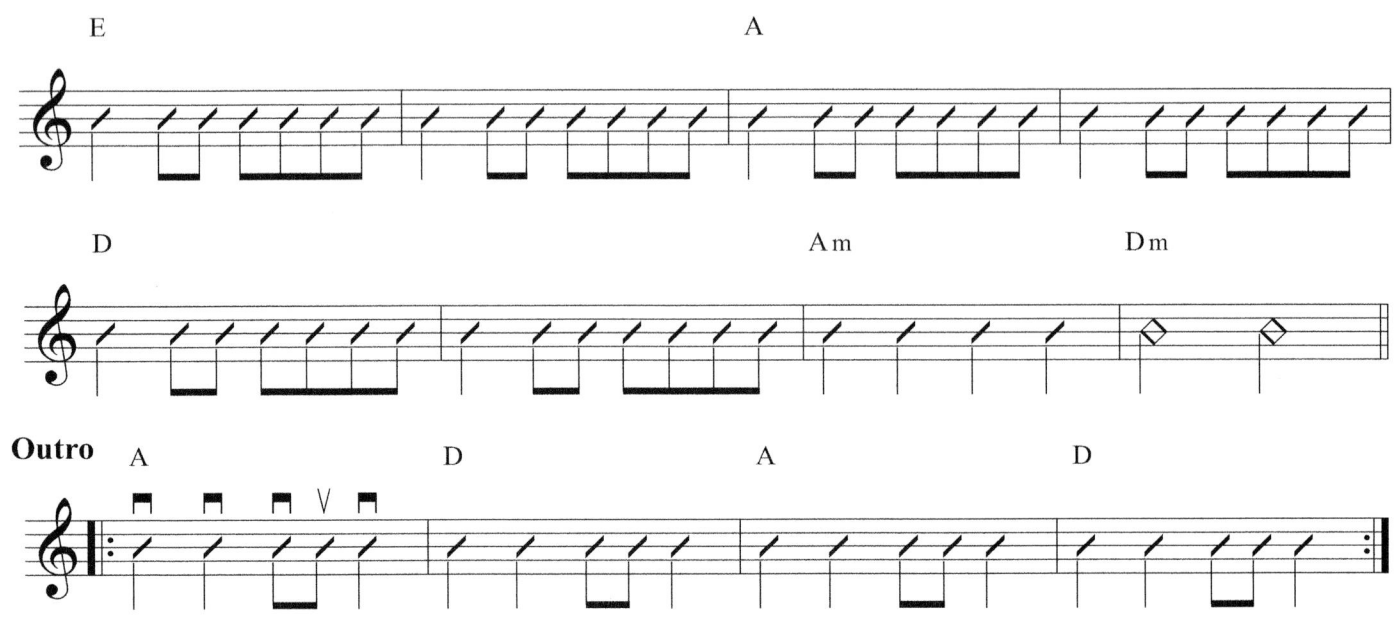

Lesson 12: Introducing Barre Chords

A **barre** means to use one finger to cover more than one fret at a time. They are often difficult to get at first, but this can be overcome with practice and patience.

Below, we will start by learning the F major chord.

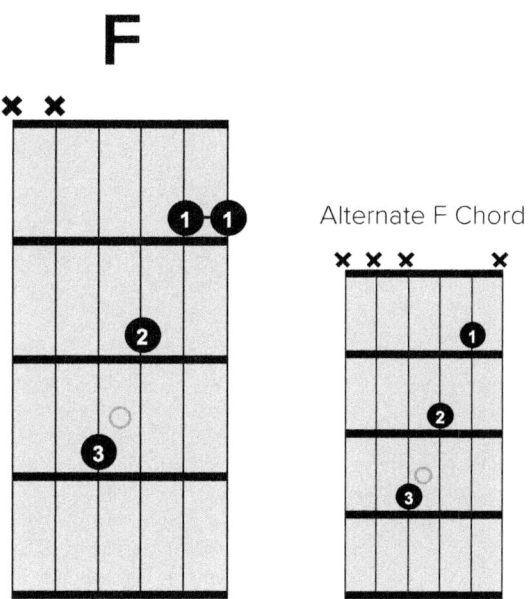

F Chord Tips:

1. Keep your fingers spread. They should not be touching each other.
2. Keep your wrist dropped, and your thumb comfortably behind the neck.
3. Your first finger should not lay flat. Instead, use a bit of the of side of your finger to get the barre. Make sure your other two fingers are high on their tips.

Try it: Practice the F chord below. If you can get at least three out of the four strings to sound, you're well on your way!

Practicing F Major

Exercise 1

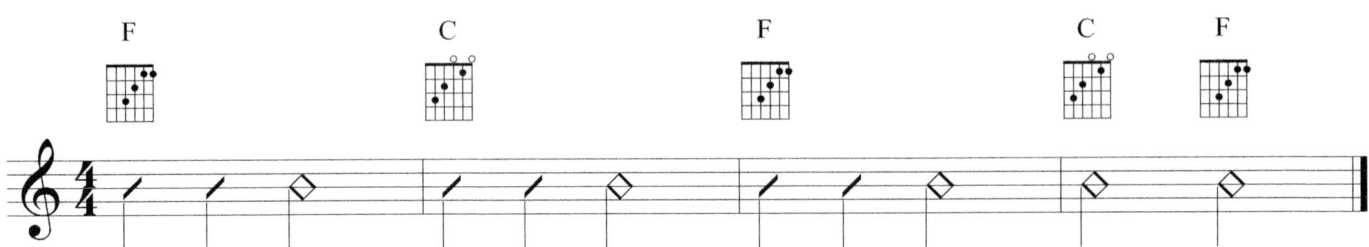

Exercise 2

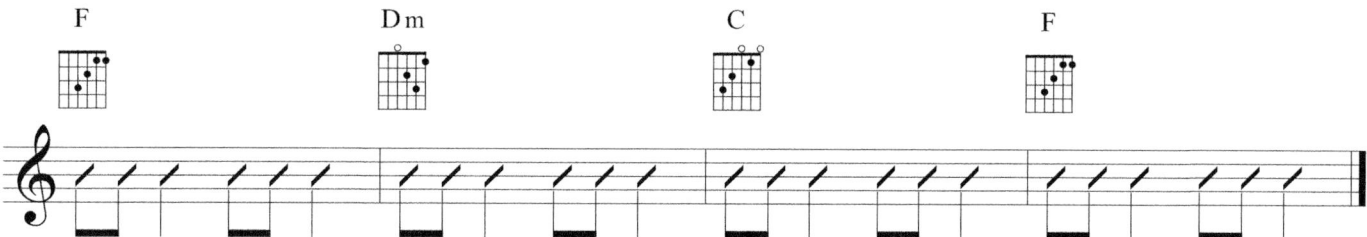

Exercise 3

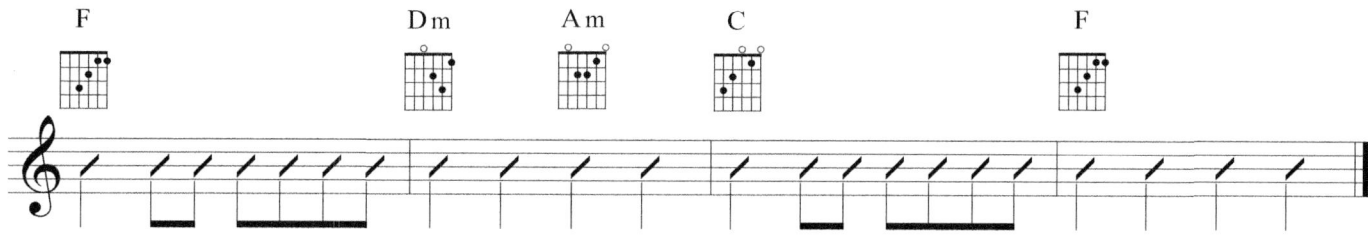

Exercise 4

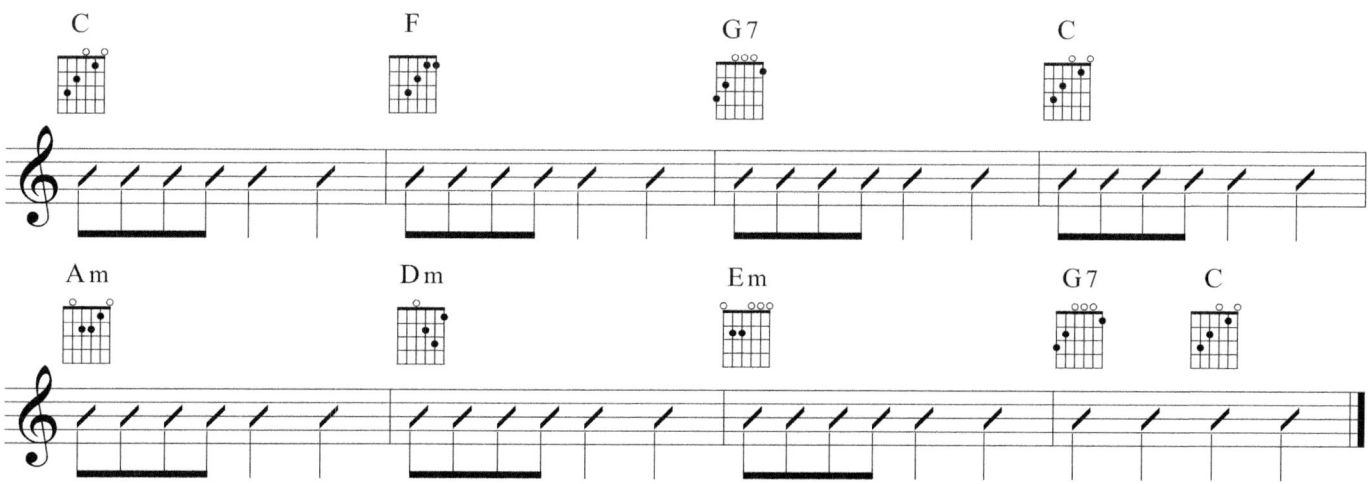

Exercise 5

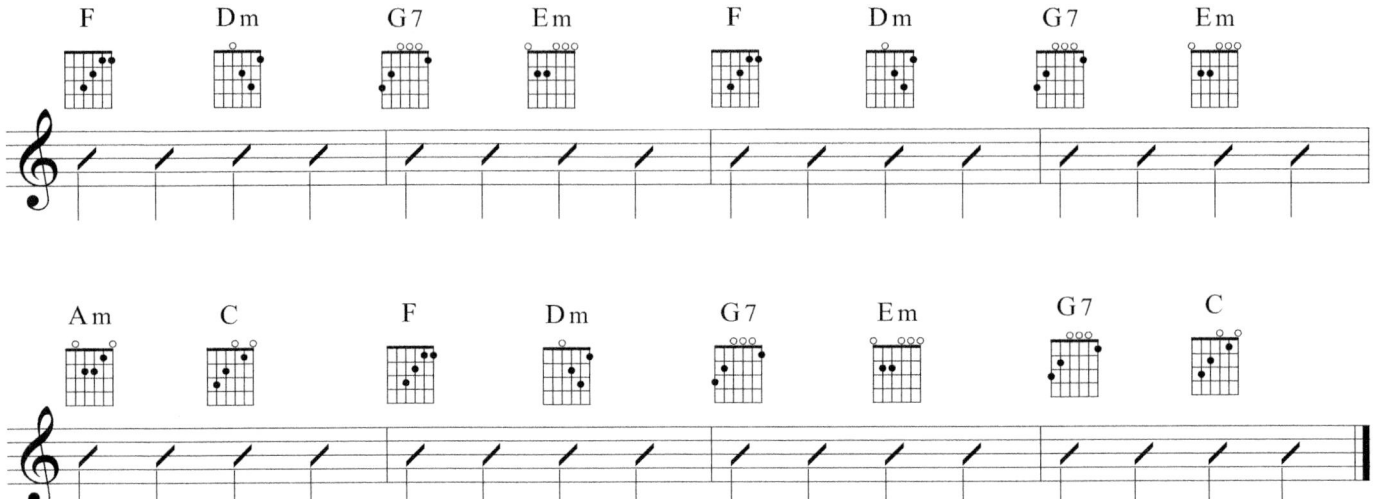

Lesson 13: 3/4 Time

In music, not everything is grouped in fours. Many times the beat will be grouped in threes instead. This is shown at the beginning of a song in the time signature.

- **Four-four time** means that you have four beats per measure and that the quarter note is the beat.

- In **three-four time**, you have three beats per measure and the quarter note is the beat here as well.

The easy way to remember it is this: in four-four count to four per measure, in three-four count to three.

Try it: Practice strumming the chords below in 3/4 time.

Tip:
Remember, for each measure, count to 3.

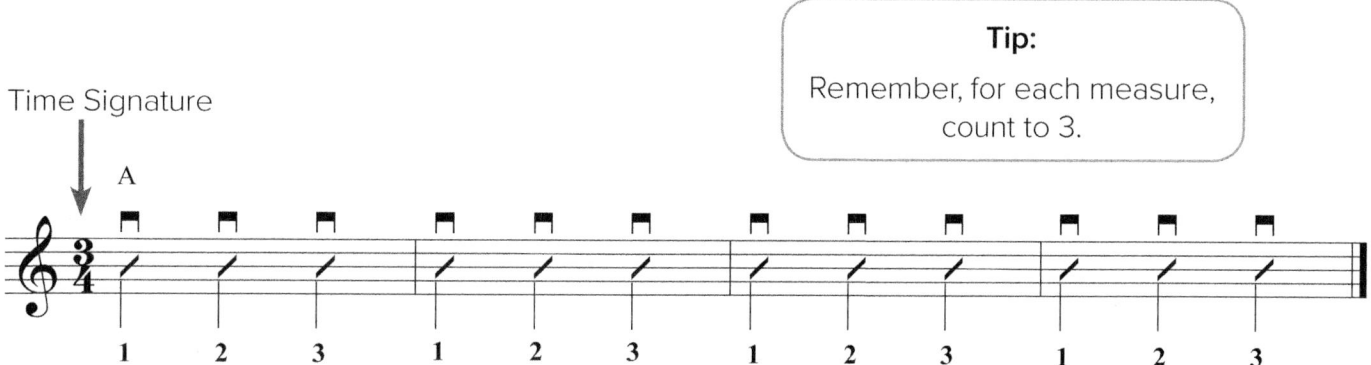

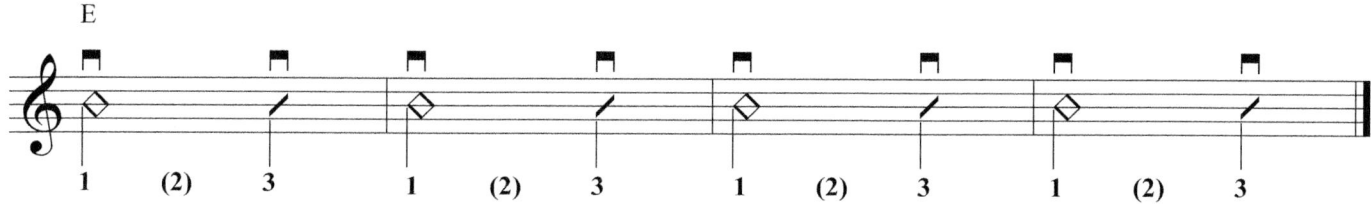

(Continued on the following page.)

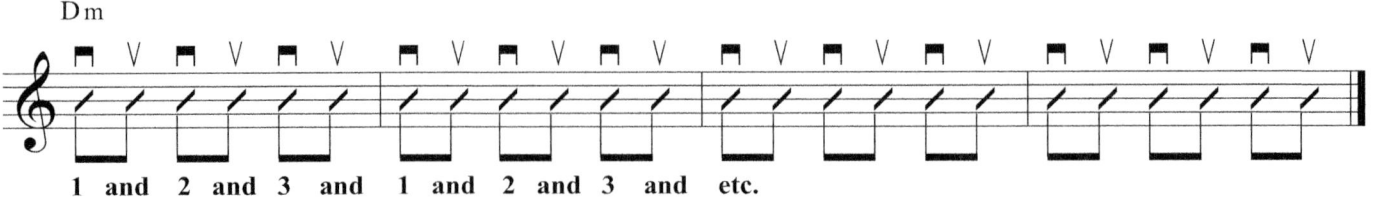

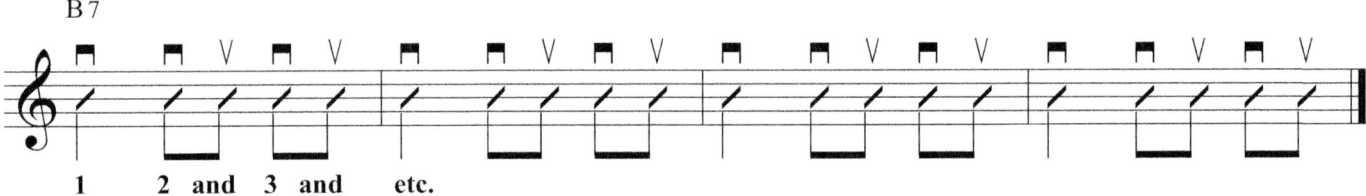

Dotted Half Notes

Since a **whole note** (worth four beats) cannot be used in three-four time, a dot is placed next to the half note, extending it to a full three beats. (See below). Note: the **dotted half note** can also be used in four-four time in the same manner.

Try it: Practice strumming the dotted half notes using the F chord.

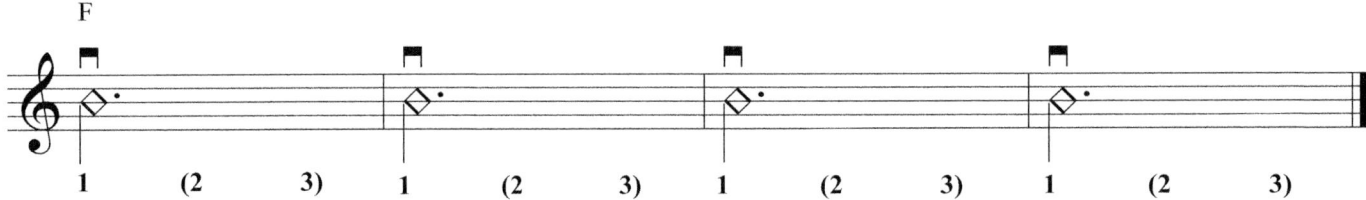

Practicing in 3/4 Time

Tip: The chord diagrams have been omitted to test your memory. See how many you can remember without looking them up. If you need a quick reference, you can find a chart of all the chords in the back of the book.

Exercise 1

Exercise 2

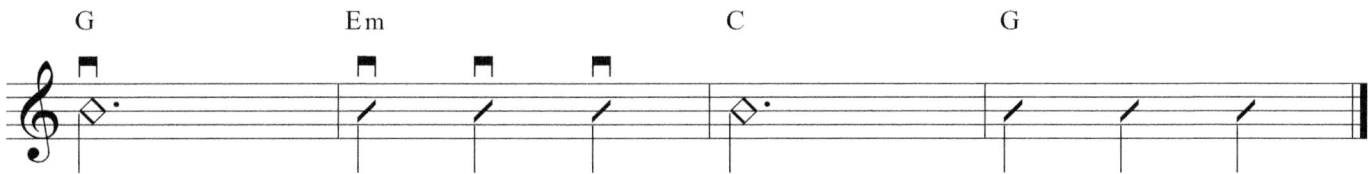

Exercise 3

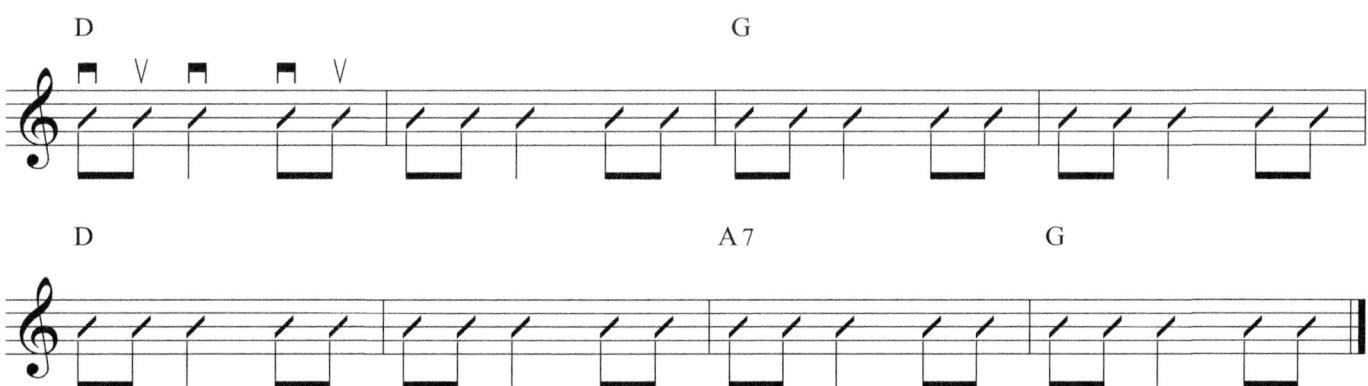

Exercise 4

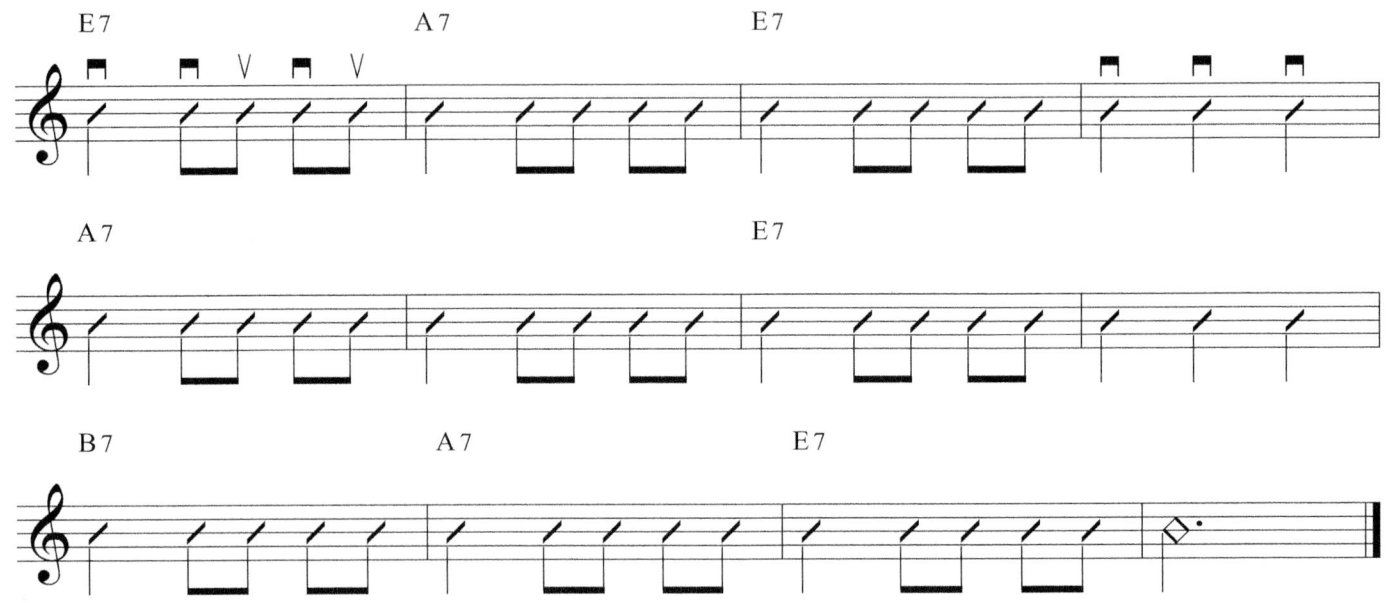

House of the Rising Sun

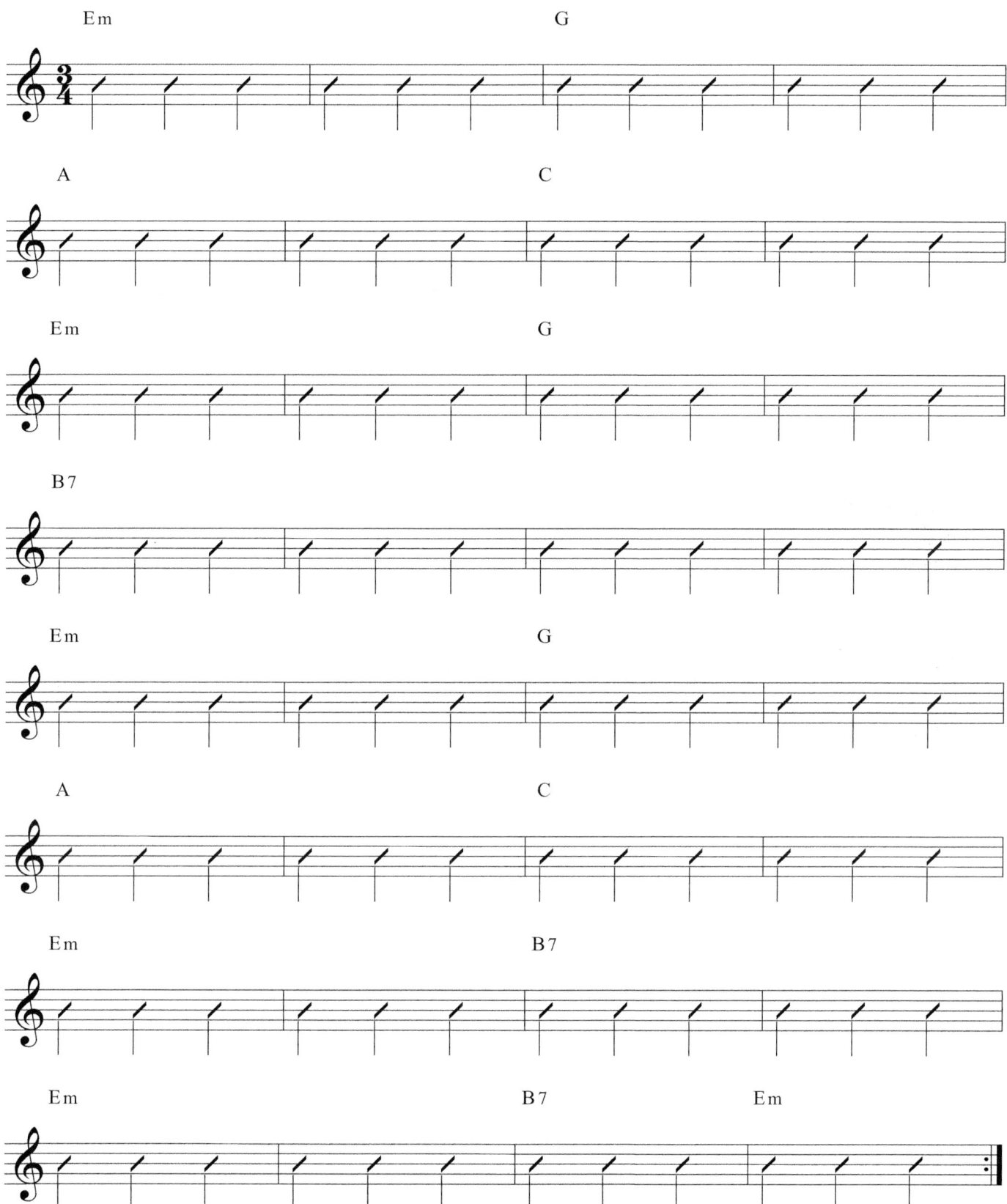

Lesson 14: B♭ Major & C7

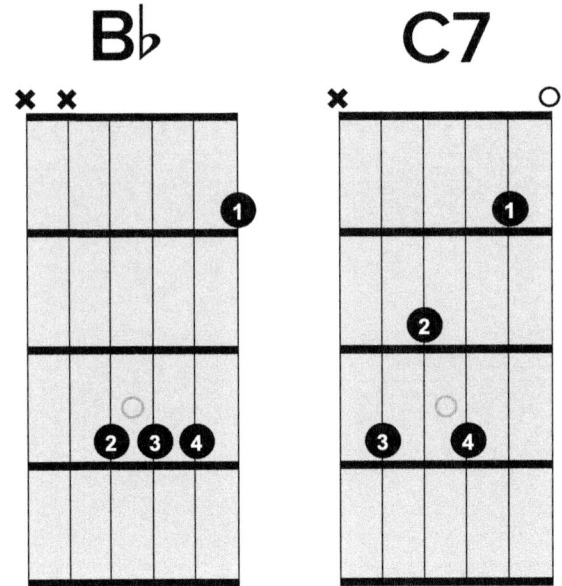

The first chord shown here is called B flat. **Flat** simply means that the note or chord is a half step lower than its natural counterpart.

Try it:

Practice the B♭ Major chord

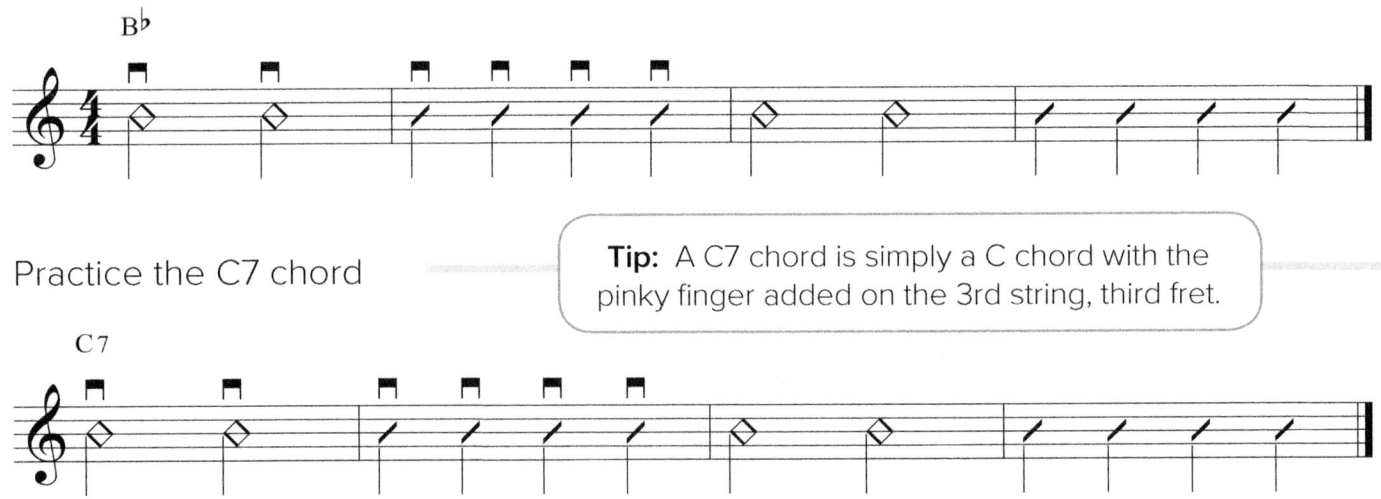

Practice the C7 chord

Tip: A C7 chord is simply a C chord with the pinky finger added on the 3rd string, third fret.

Practice the B♭ and the C7 chords in 3/4 time

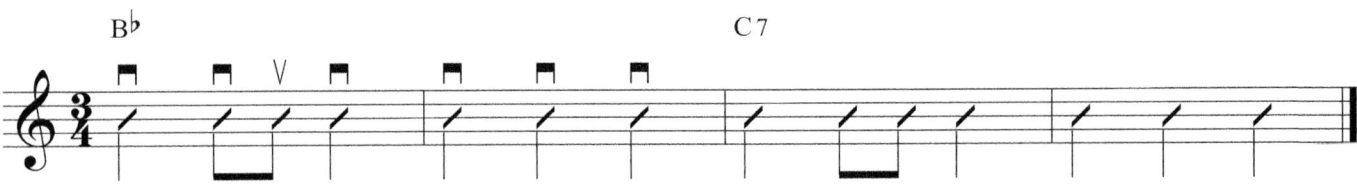

Practicing B♭, C7, and F

Exercise 1

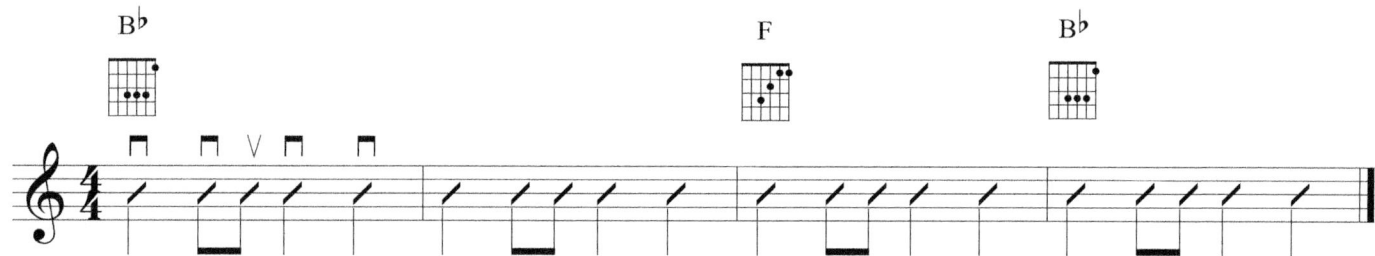

Exercise 2

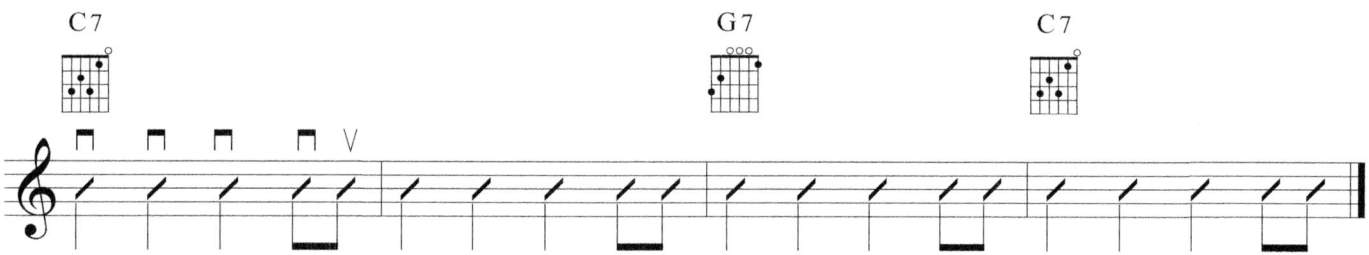

Exercise 3

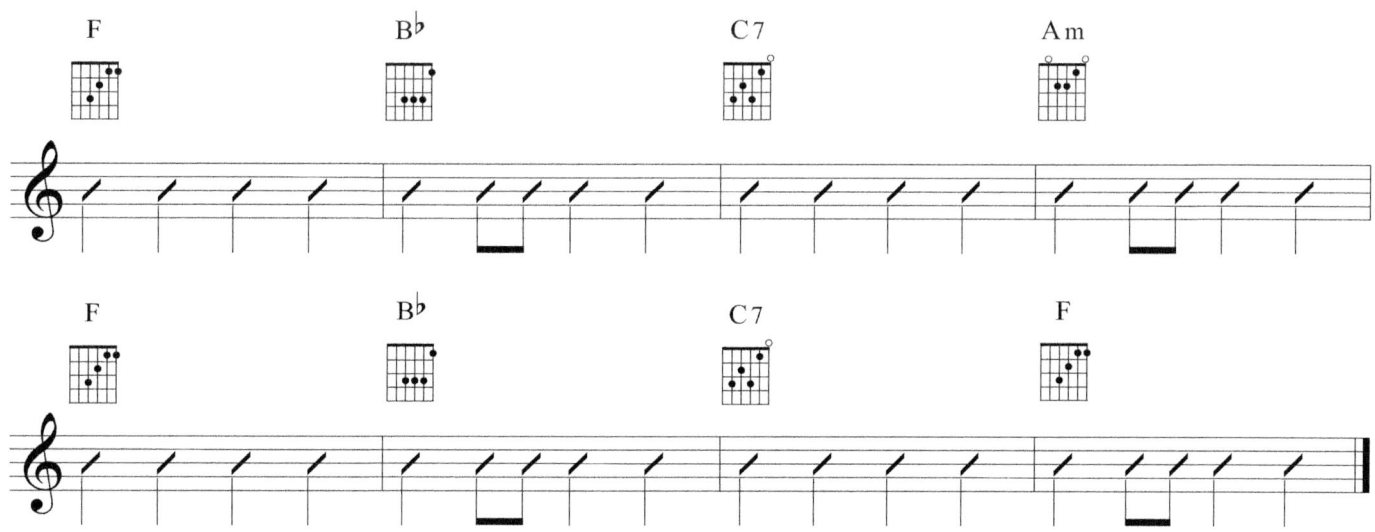

Exercise 4

Tip:
Note the change to 3/4 time.

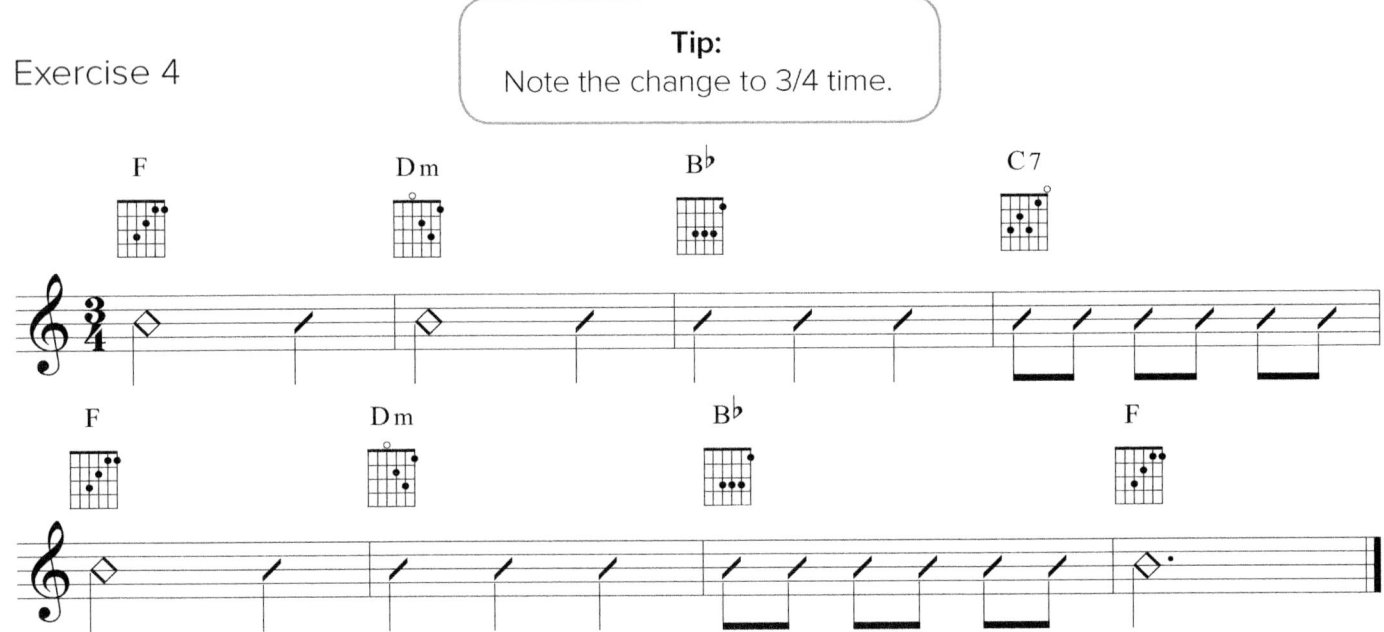

Exercise 5

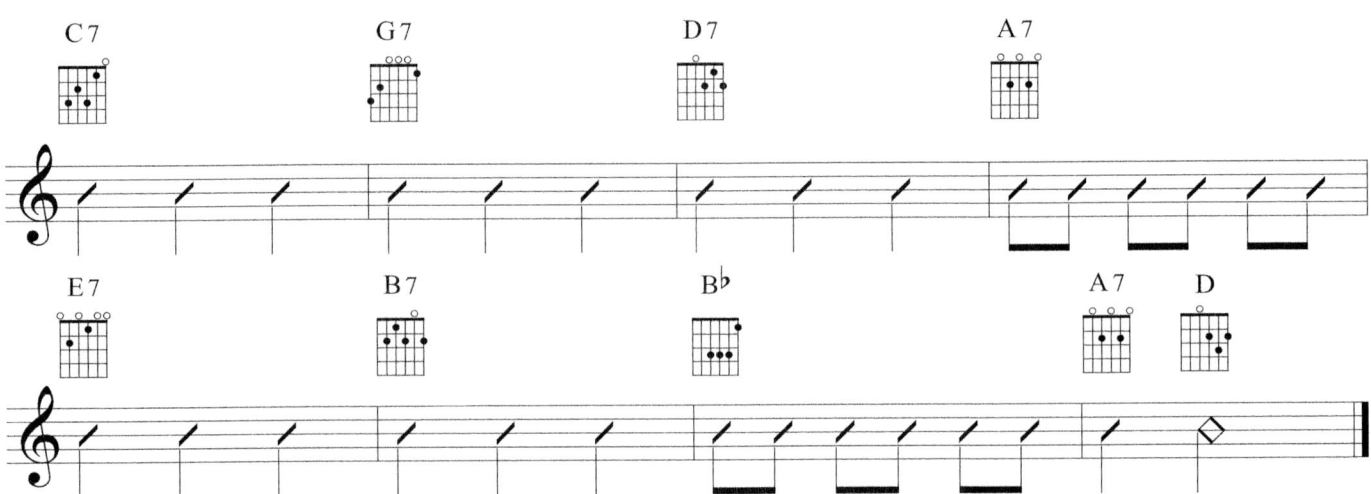

Berry's Blues

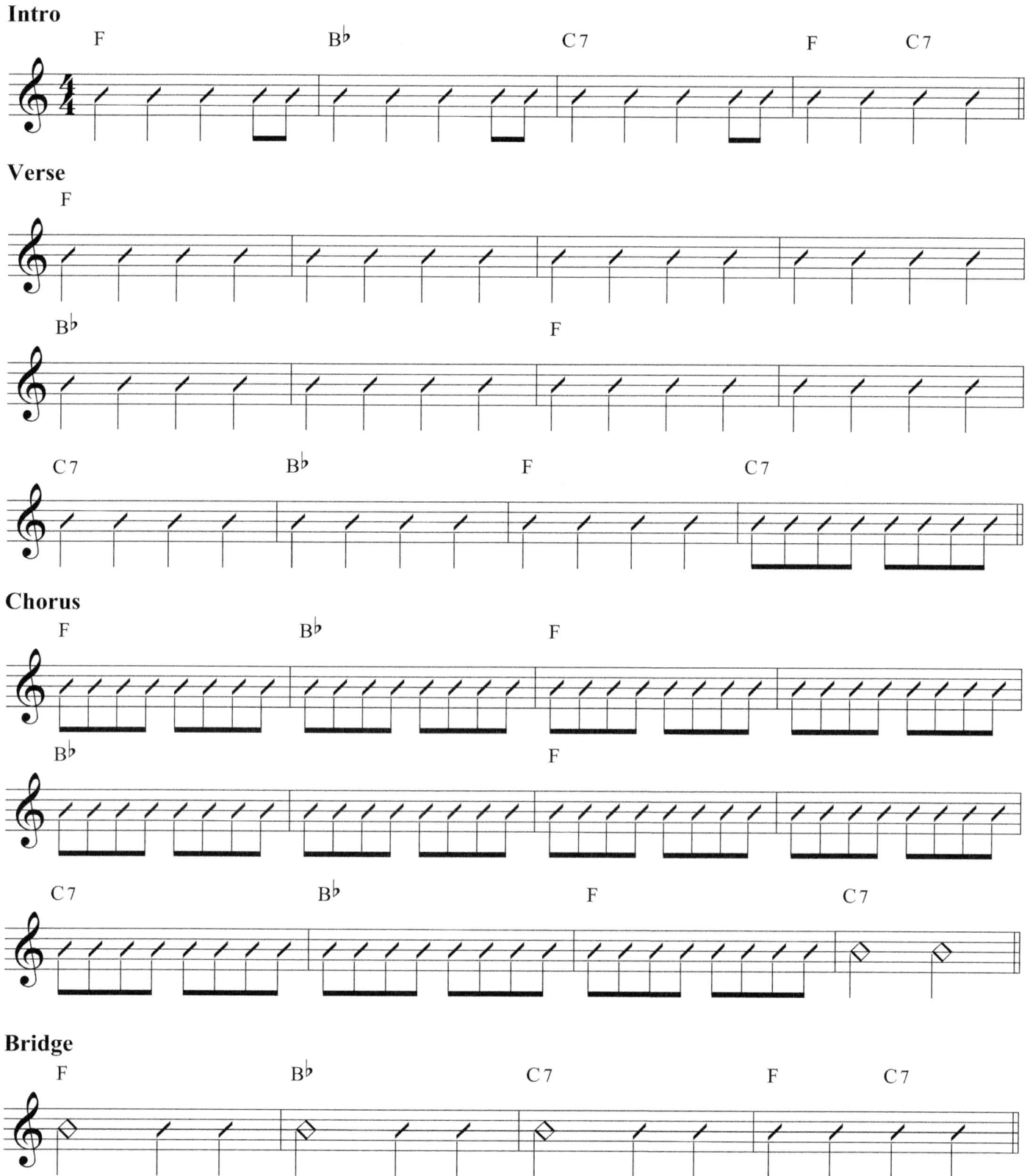

Verse

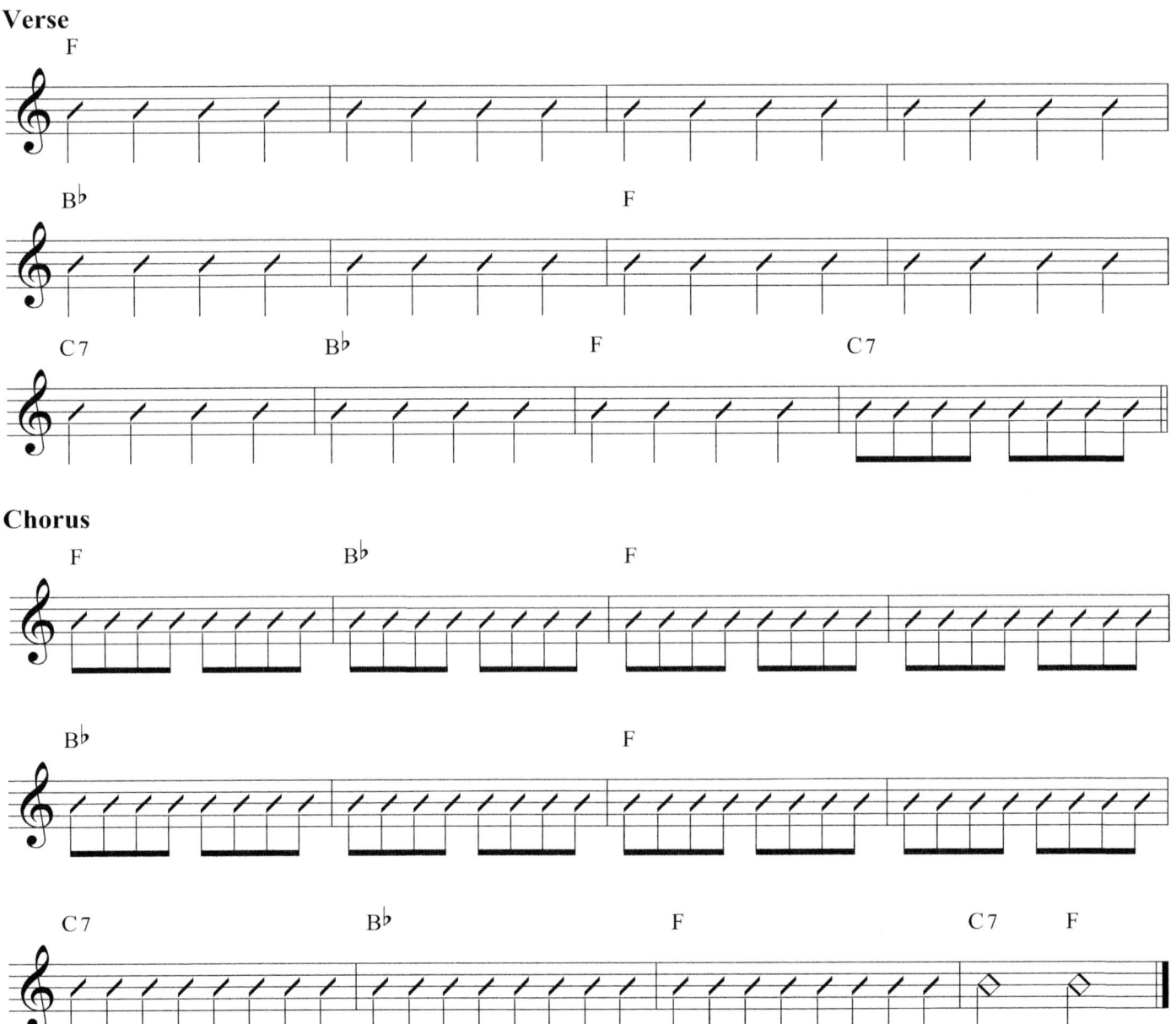

Chorus

Lesson 15: Introducing Minor Barre Chords

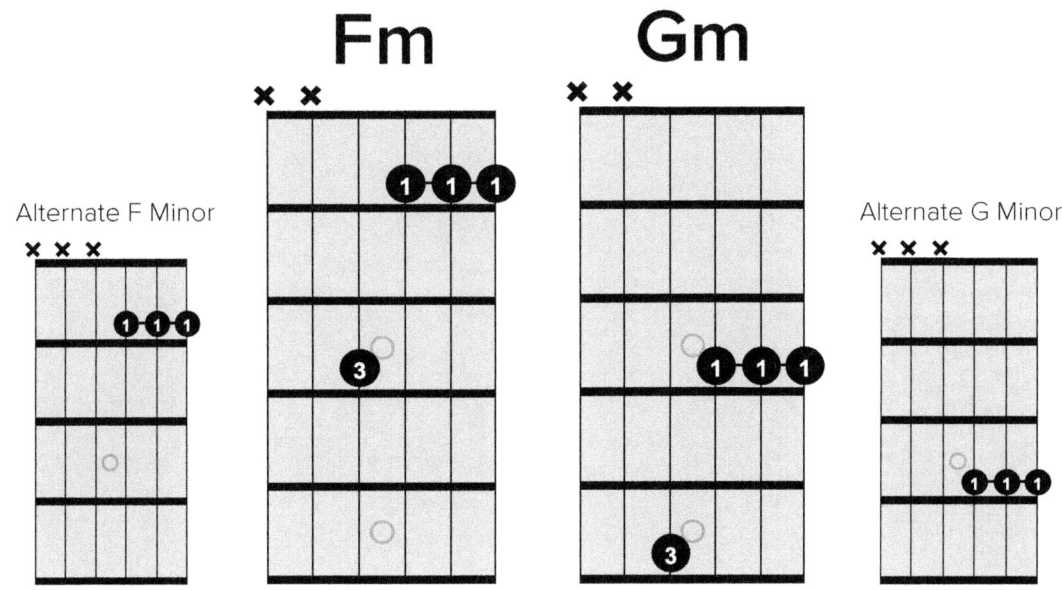

Try it:

Practice the F minor chord

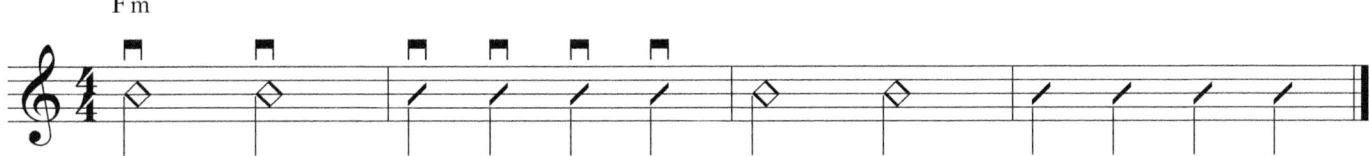

Practice the G minor chord

Practice the F minor and G minor chords in 3/4 time

Practicing Fm & Gm in 4/4 Time

Exercise 1:

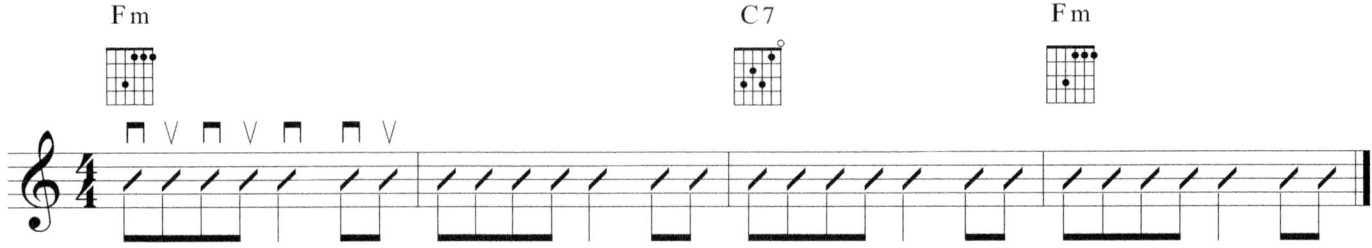

Exercise 2:

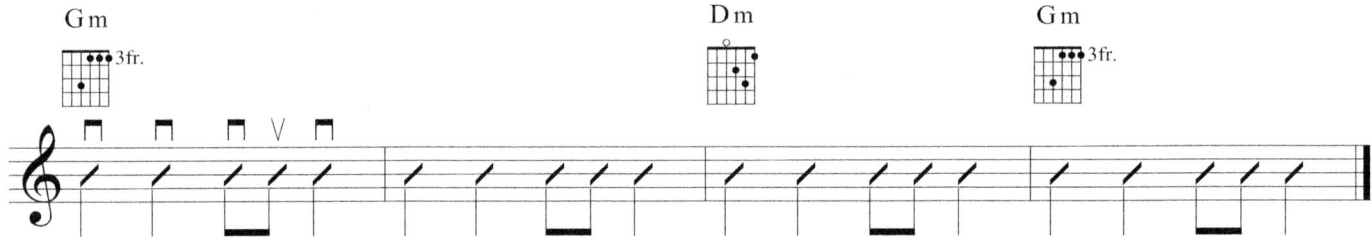

Exercise 3:

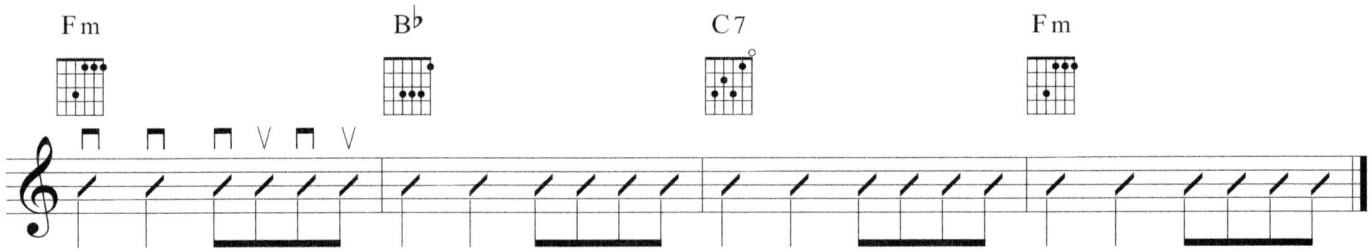

Exercise 4:

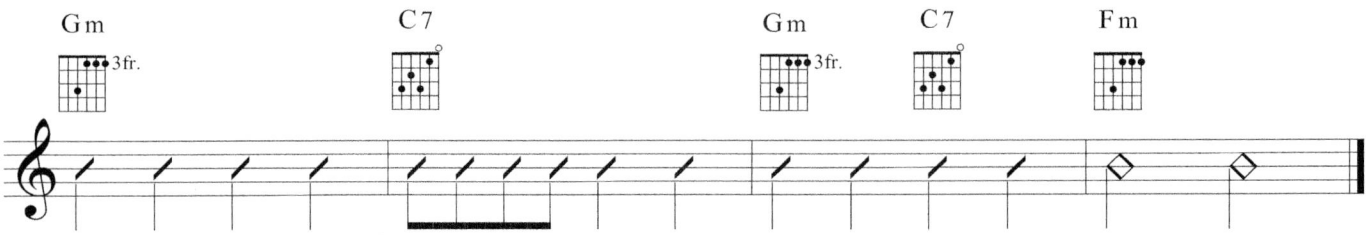

Practicing Fm & Gm in 3/4 Time

Exercise 1:

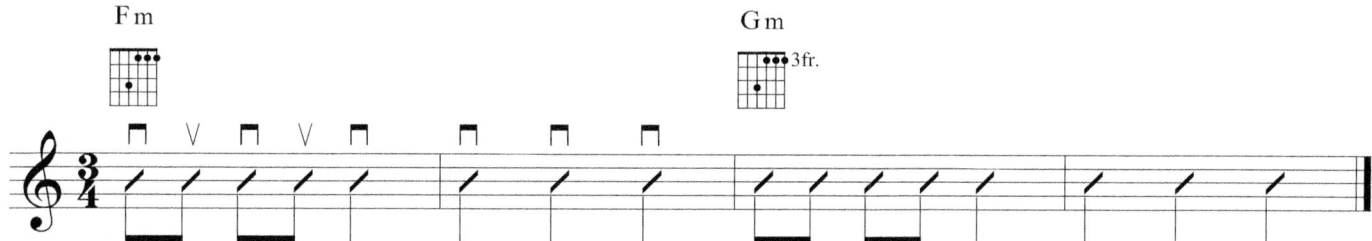

Exercise 2:

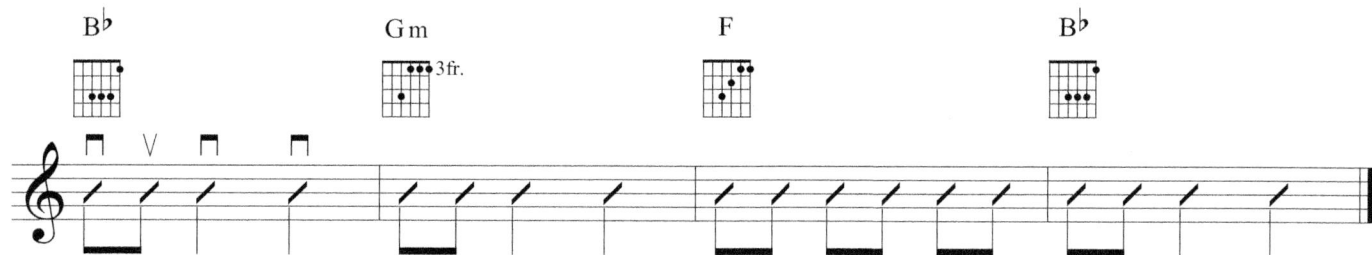

Exercise 3:

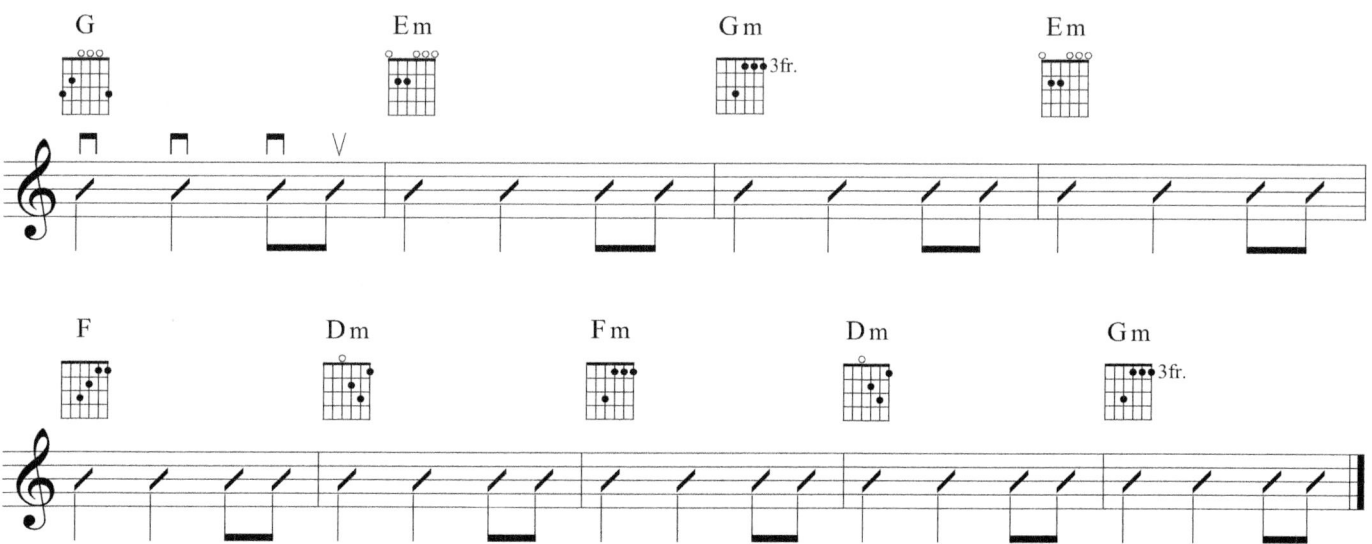

Lesson 16: B Minor & C Minor

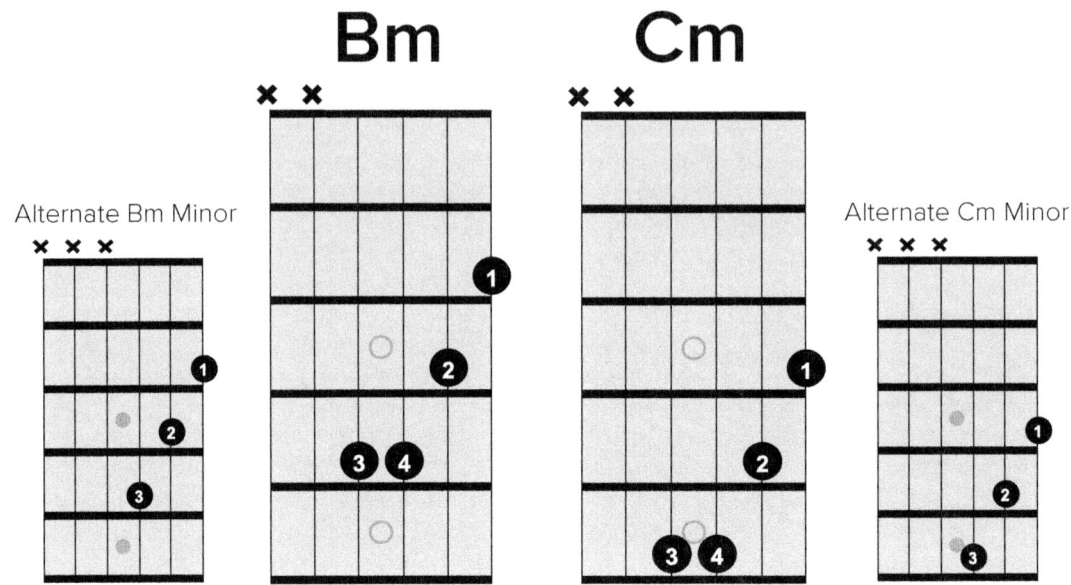

Try it: Practice the B minor and C minor chords using the rhythms below.

Practice the B minor chord

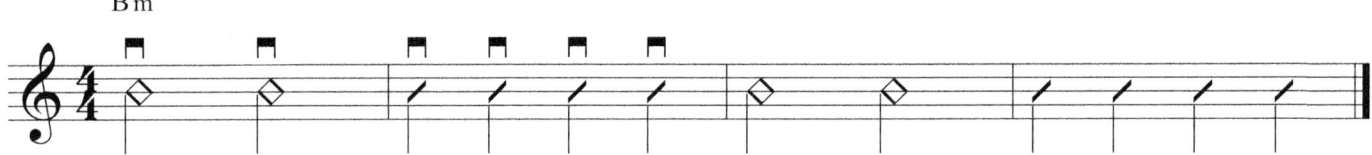

Practice the C minor chord

Practice the B minor and C minor chords in 3/4 time

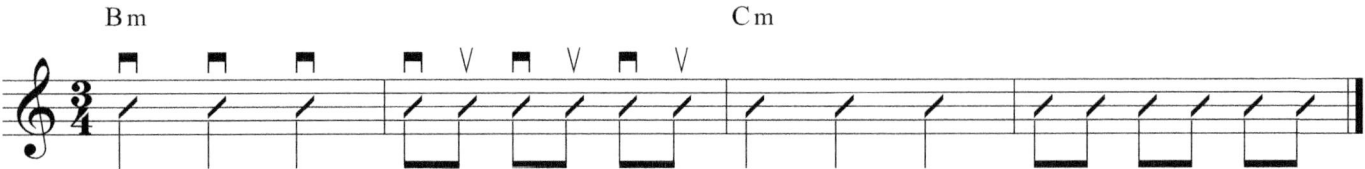

Practicing Bm & Cm

Exercise 1: Practice Bm and Cm in 4/4 time.

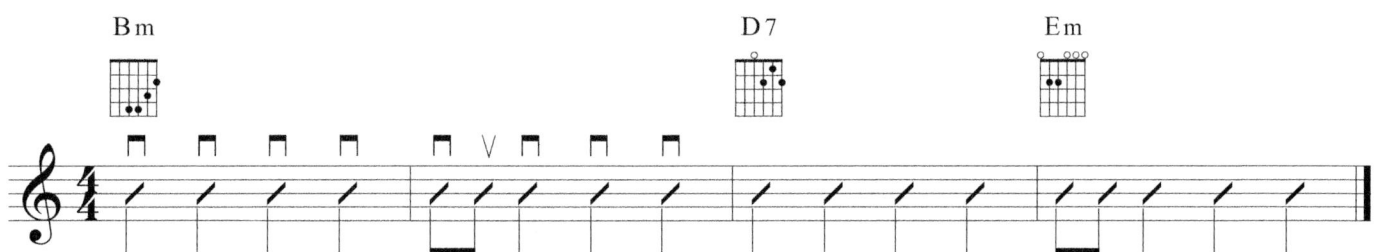

Exercise 2

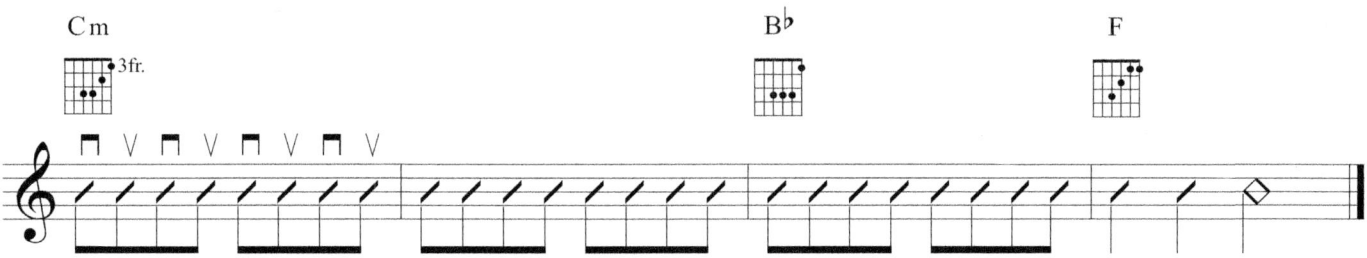

Exercise 3

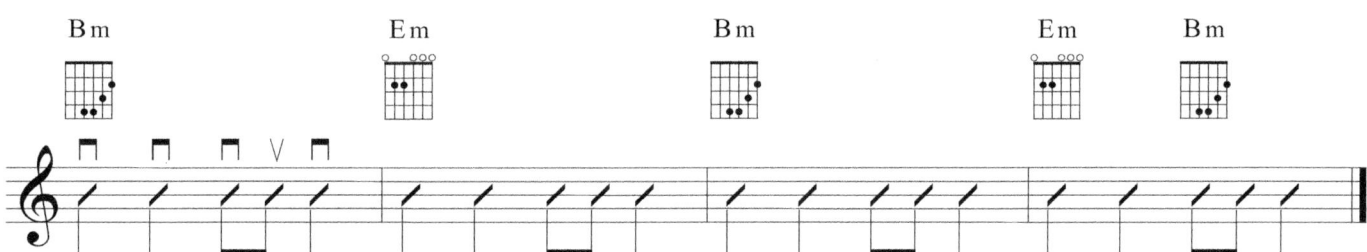

Exercise 4

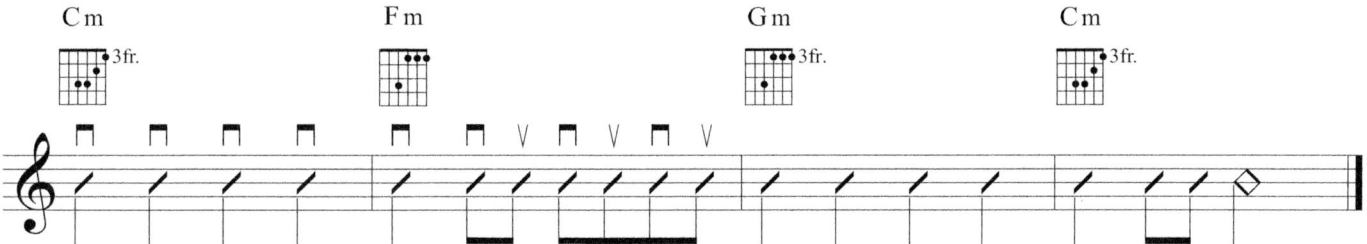

Exercise 5: Practice Bm and Cm in 3/4 time.

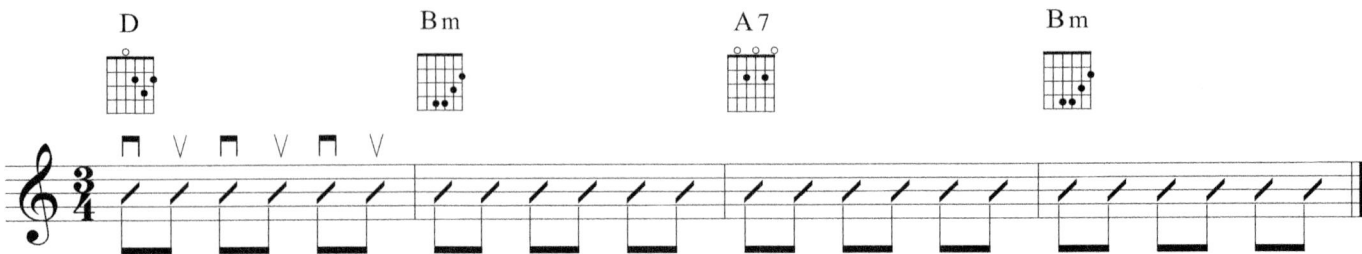

Exercise 6

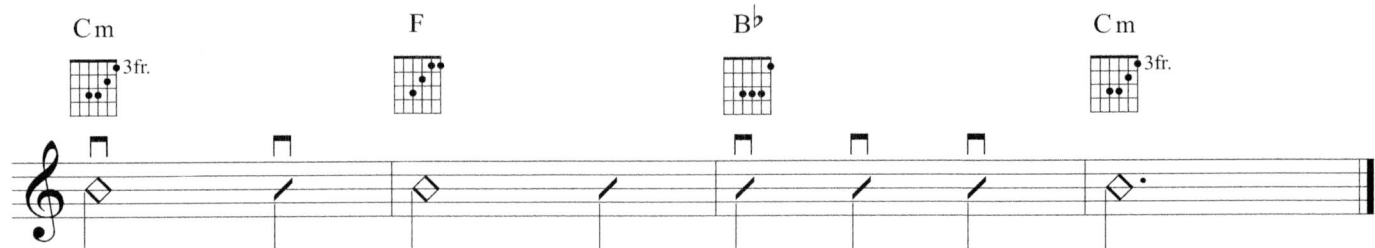

Exercise 7

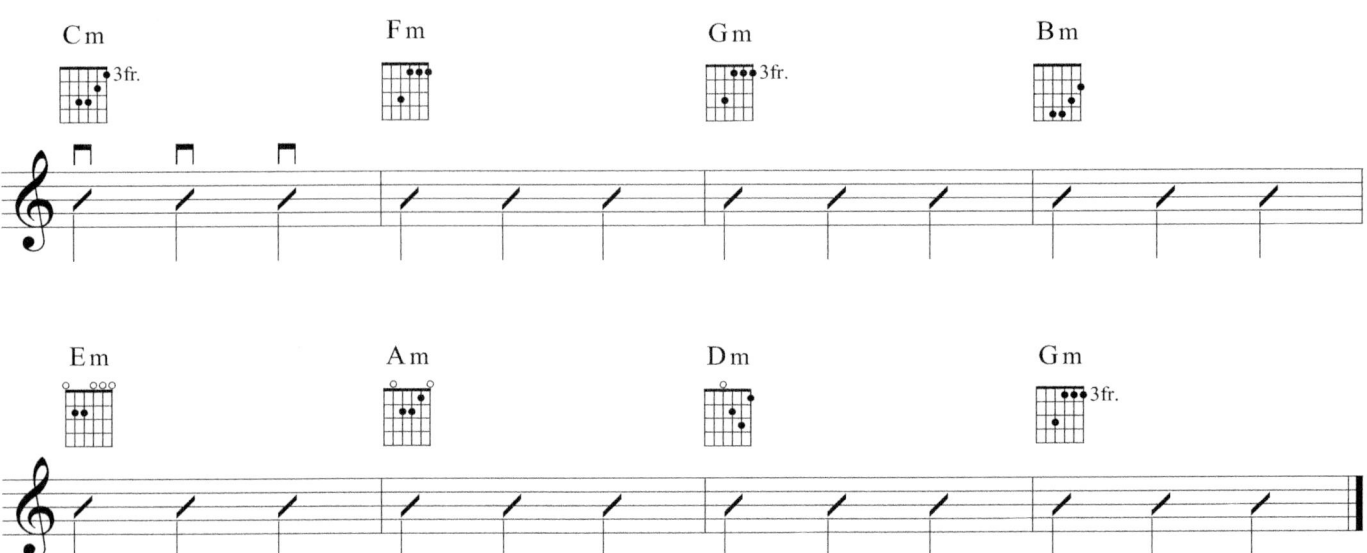

Lesson 17: Ties & Rests

Ties

A **tie** is a curved line that connects two rhythms together in order to extend the length of the rhythm. So when you see a tie, you strum the first note of the tie, but not the second one. (See below.)

Try it: Practice playing ties using the rhythms below.

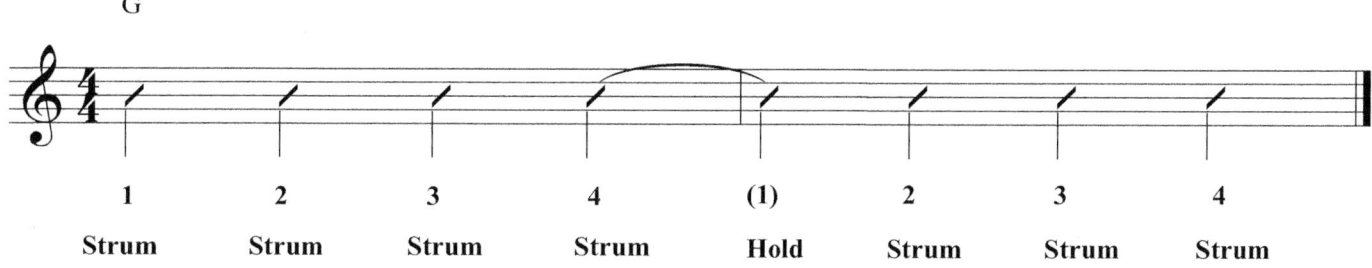

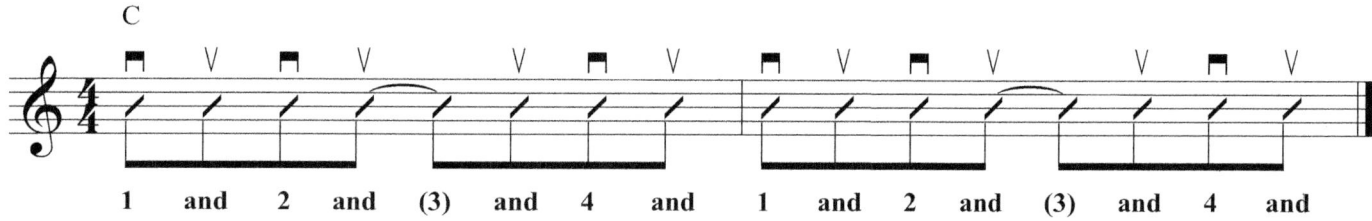

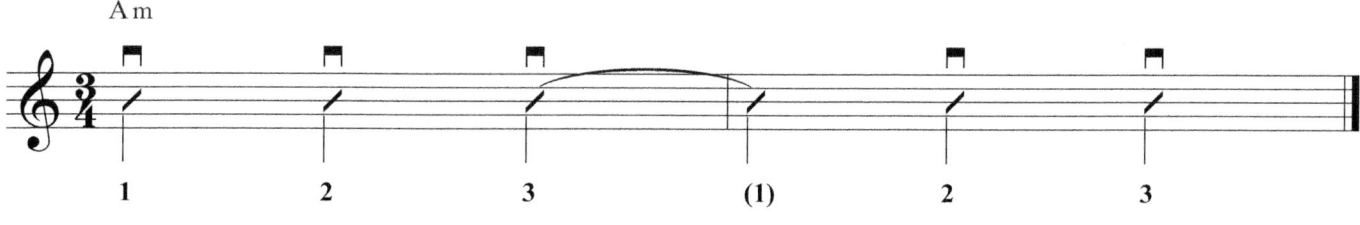

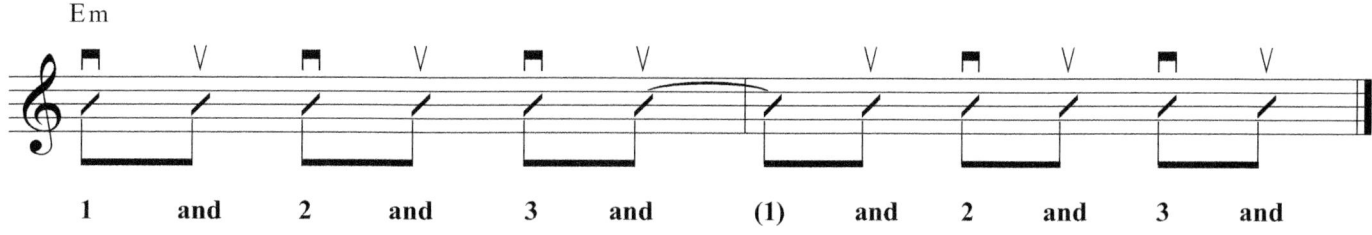

Rests

Rests are short moments of silence in music. They can give pieces of music much needed space, places to breathe, so to speak. When playing them on guitar, a rest means that you have to stop the sound of the guitar for the duration of the rest. This can be accomplished by placing the picking hand over the strings to stop the sound. In some cases you can also use the fretting hand to stop the sound.

Each rhythmic value has a corresponding rest, as shown below.

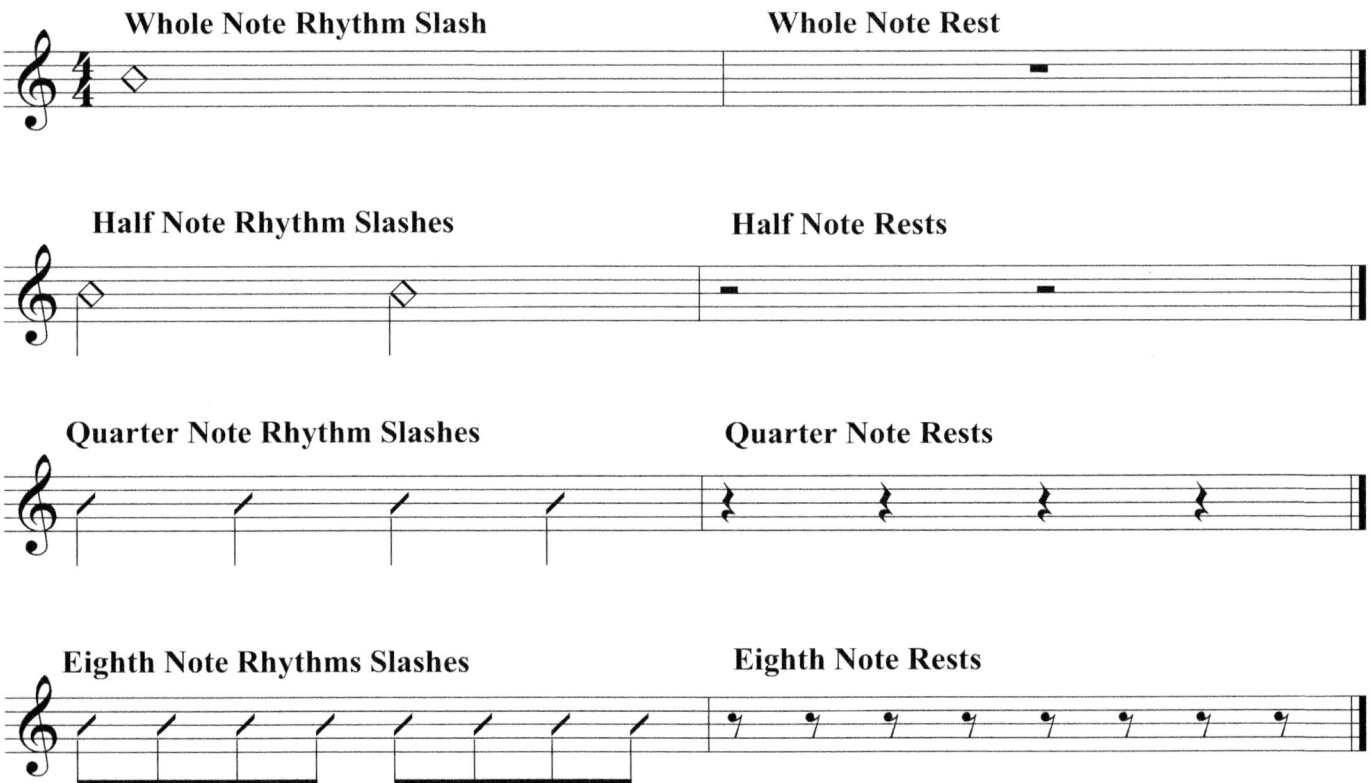

Practicing Ties & Rests

Exercise 1

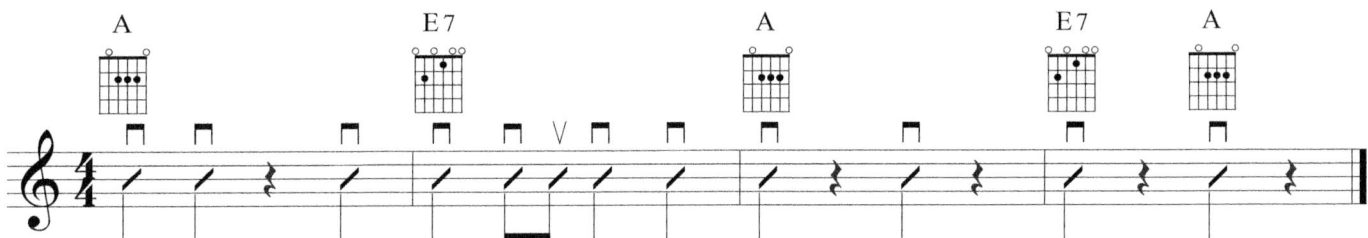

Exercise 2

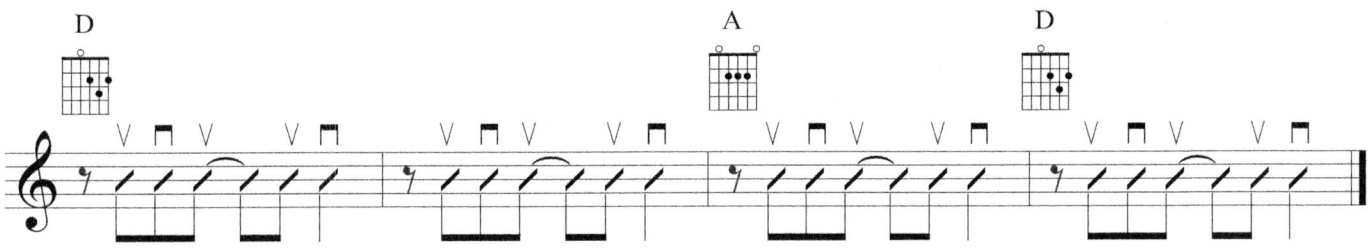

Exercise 3

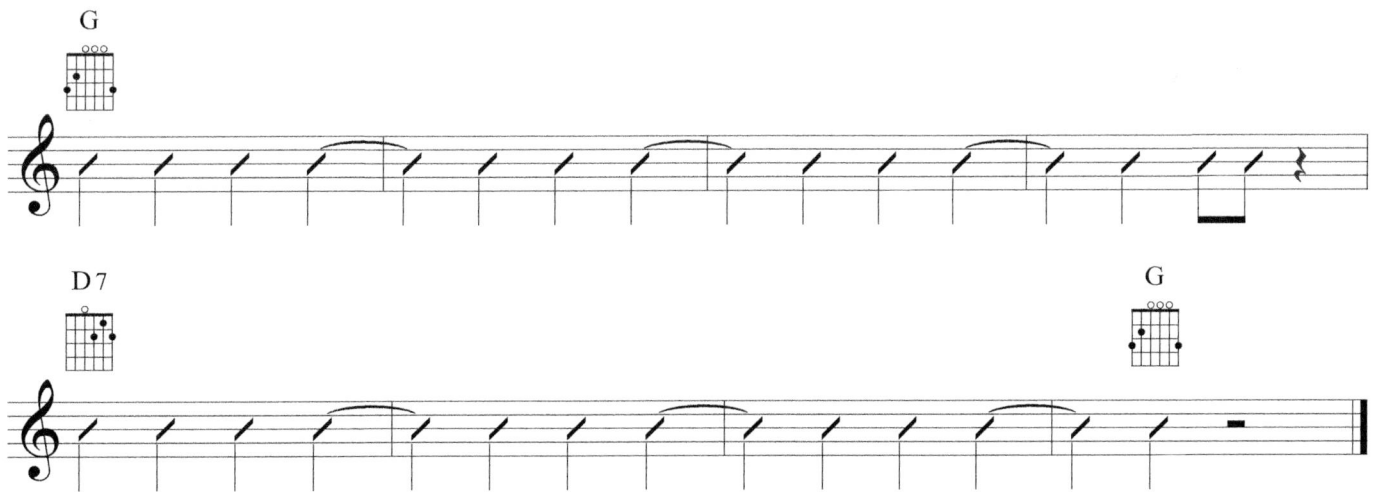

Exercise 4

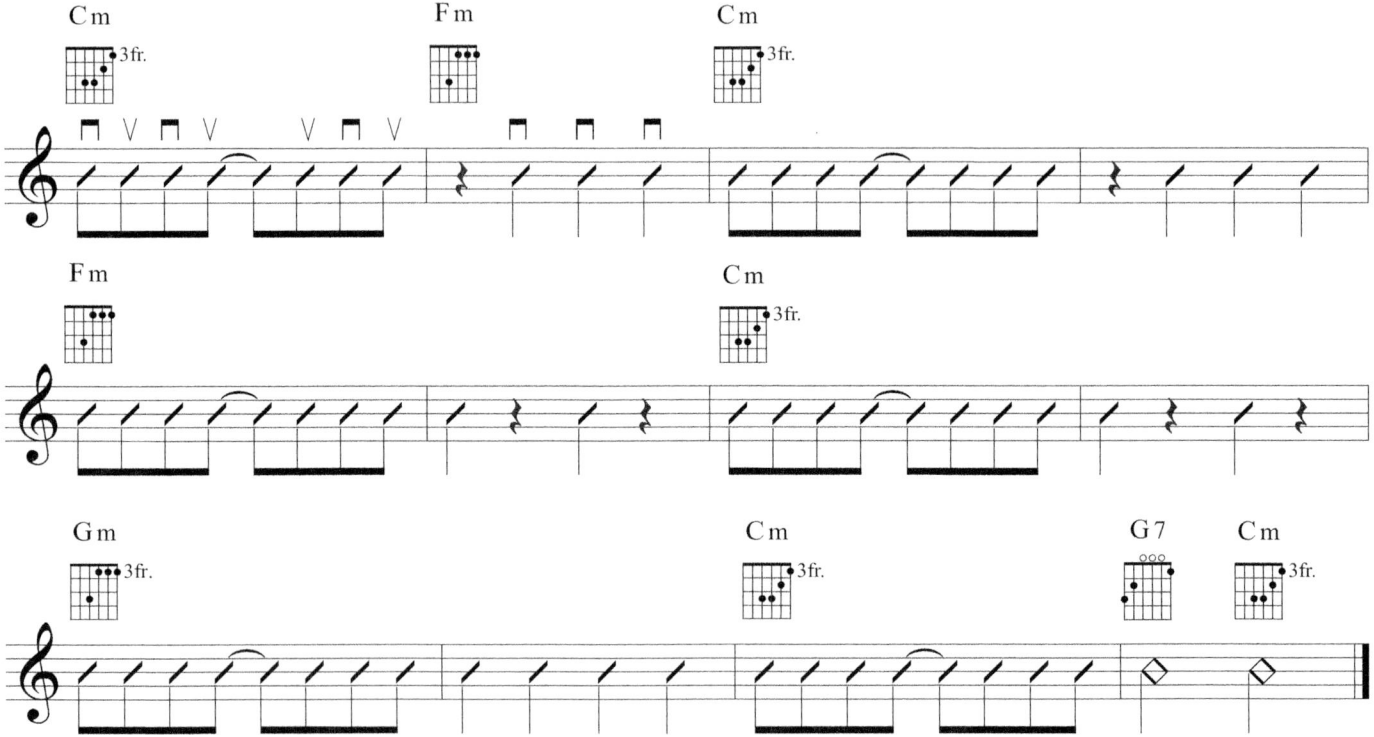

Exercise 5

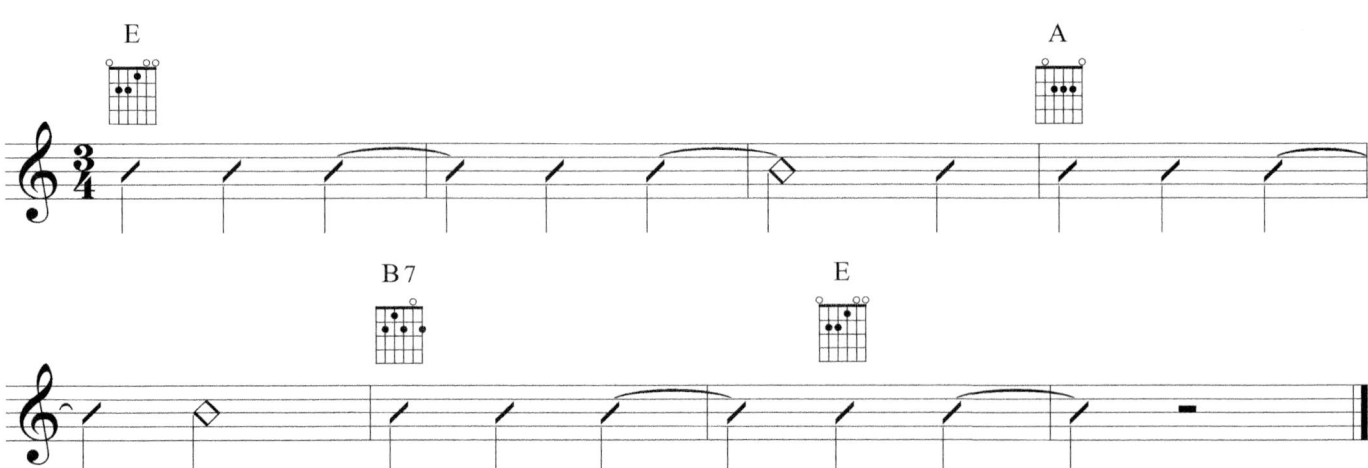

Exercise 6

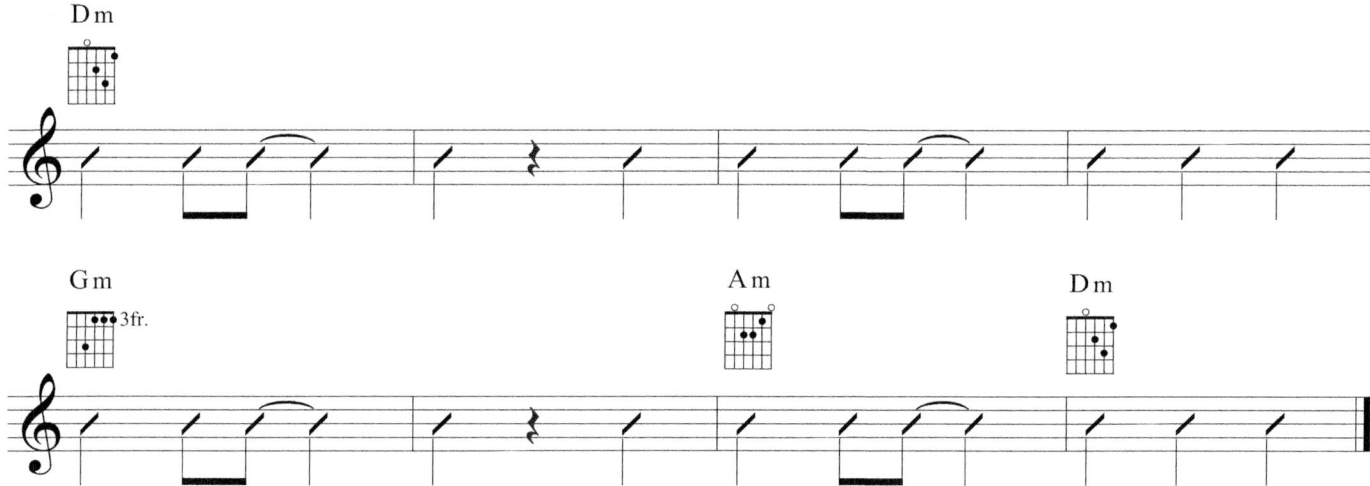

The Playground

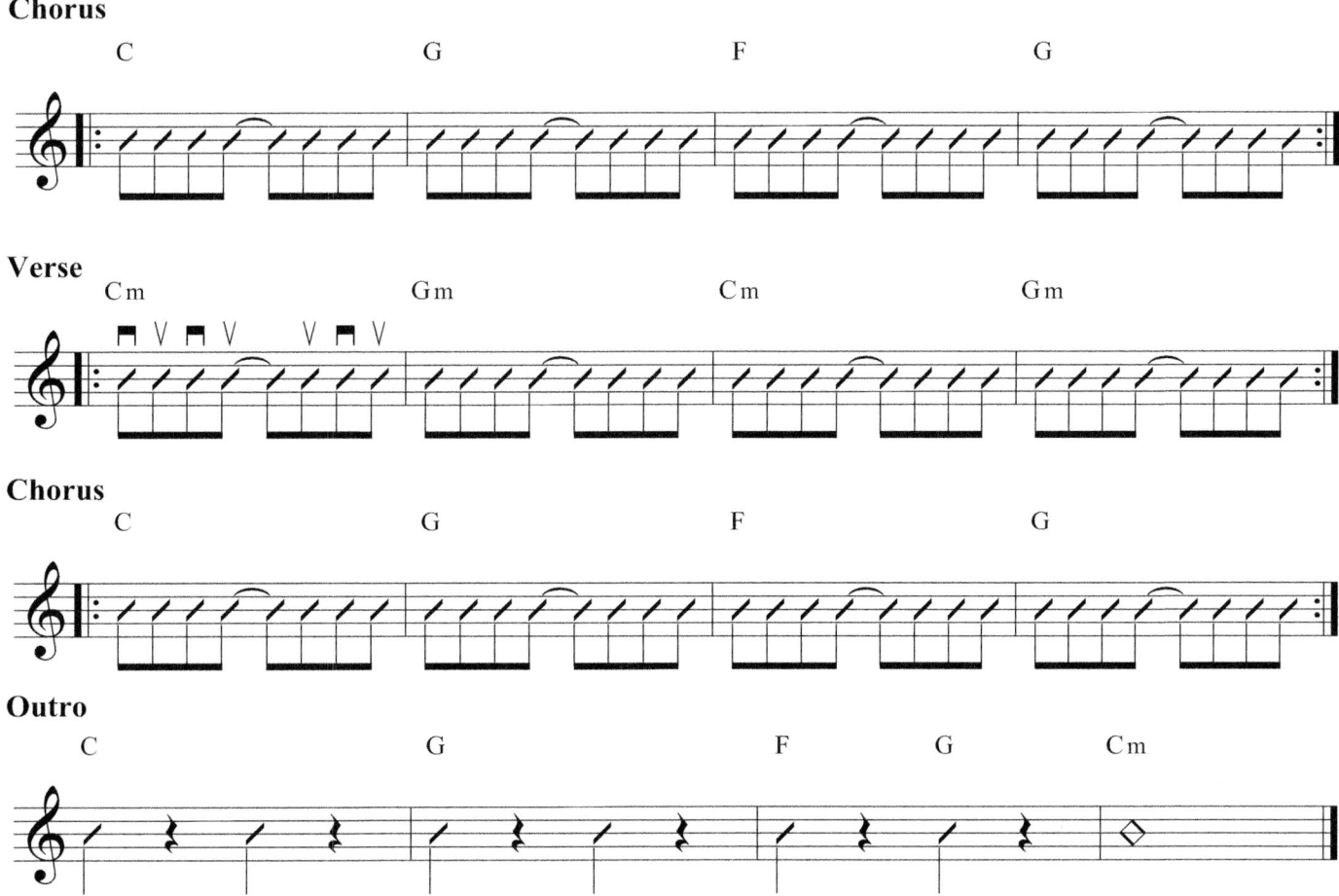

Lesson 18: F# Minor

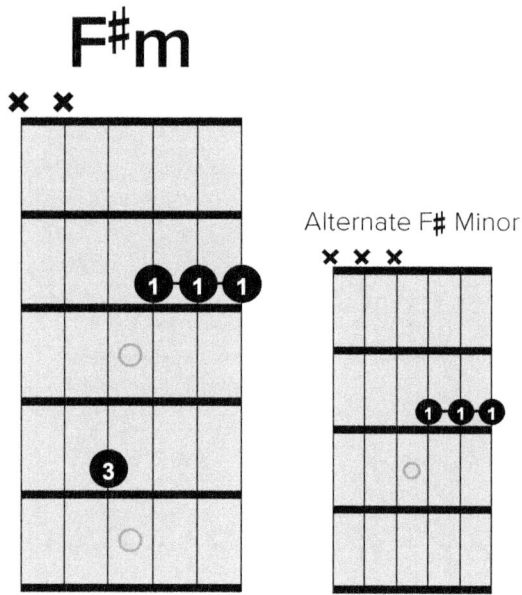

The chord shown here is called F sharp minor. **Sharp** simply means that the note or chord is a half step higher than its natural counterpart.

Try it: Practice the F# minor chord using the rhythms below.

Practice the F# minor chord in 4/4 time

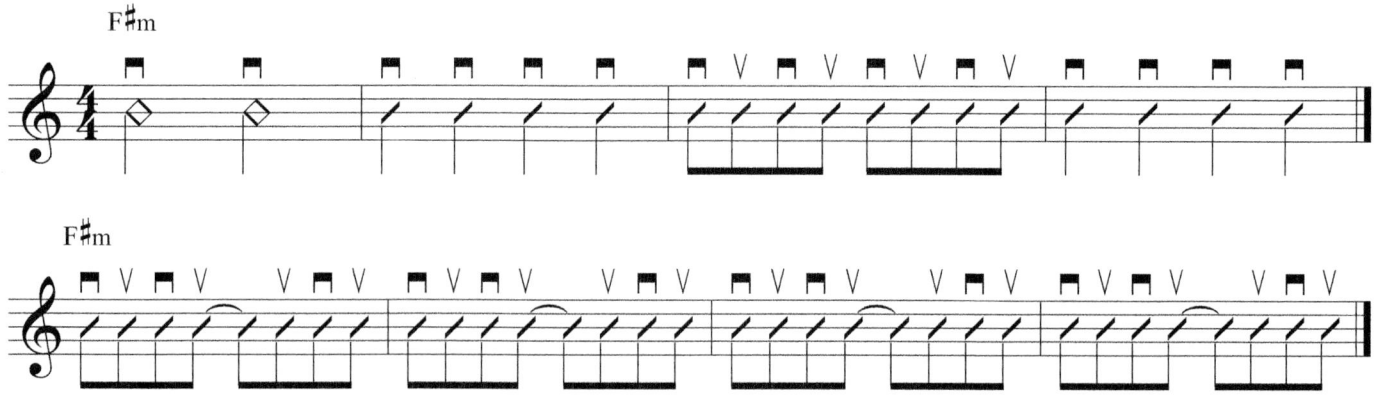

Practice the F# minor chord in 3/4 time

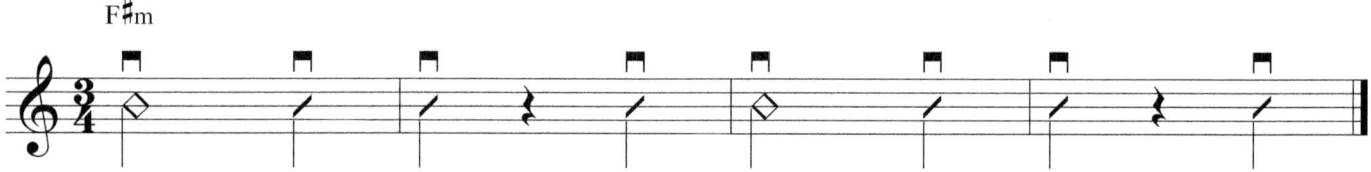

Practicing F# Minor

Exercise 1

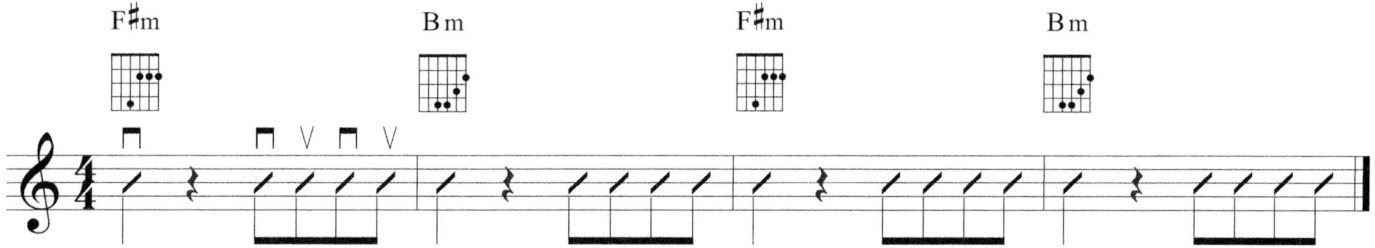

Exercise 2

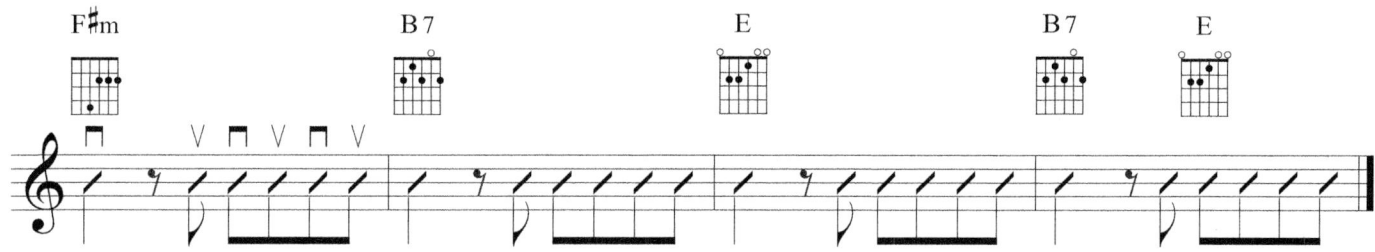

Exercise 3

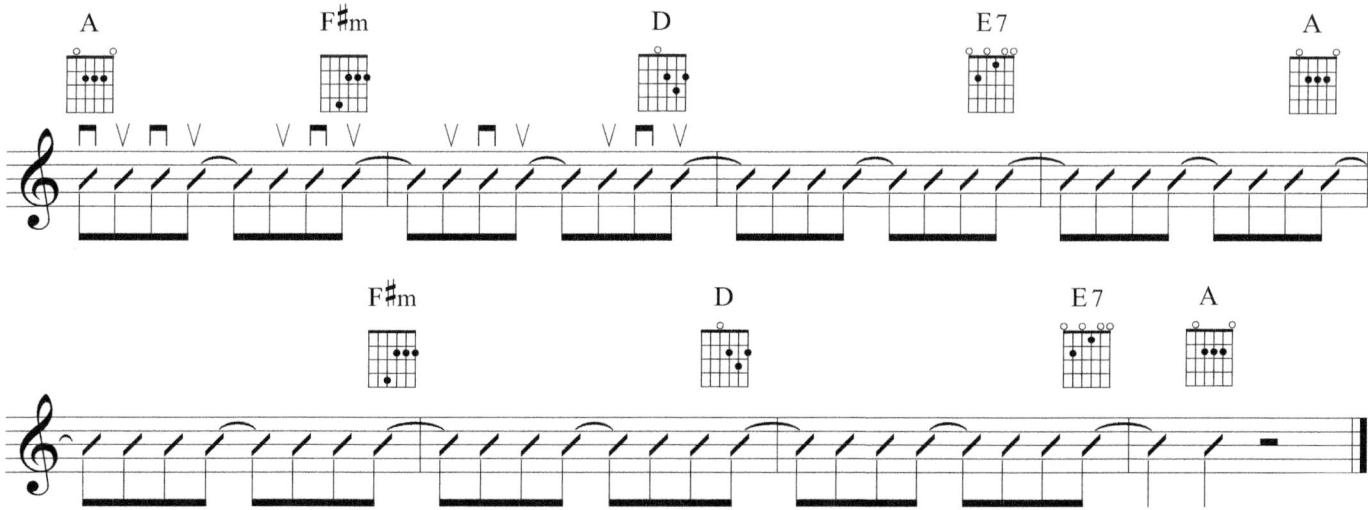

Exercise 4

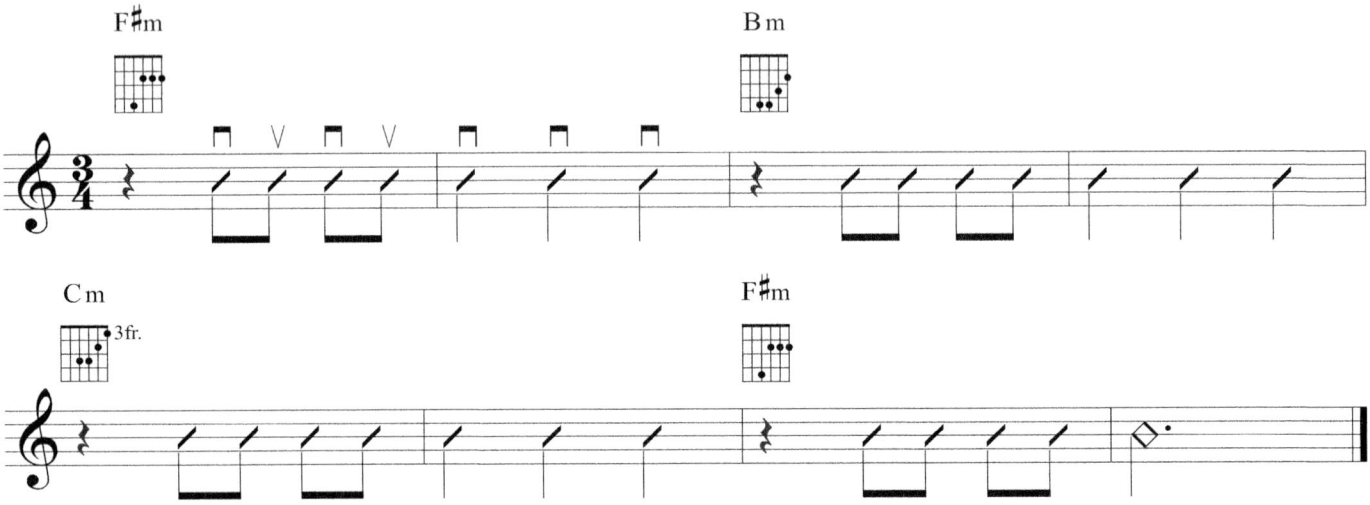

Exercise 5

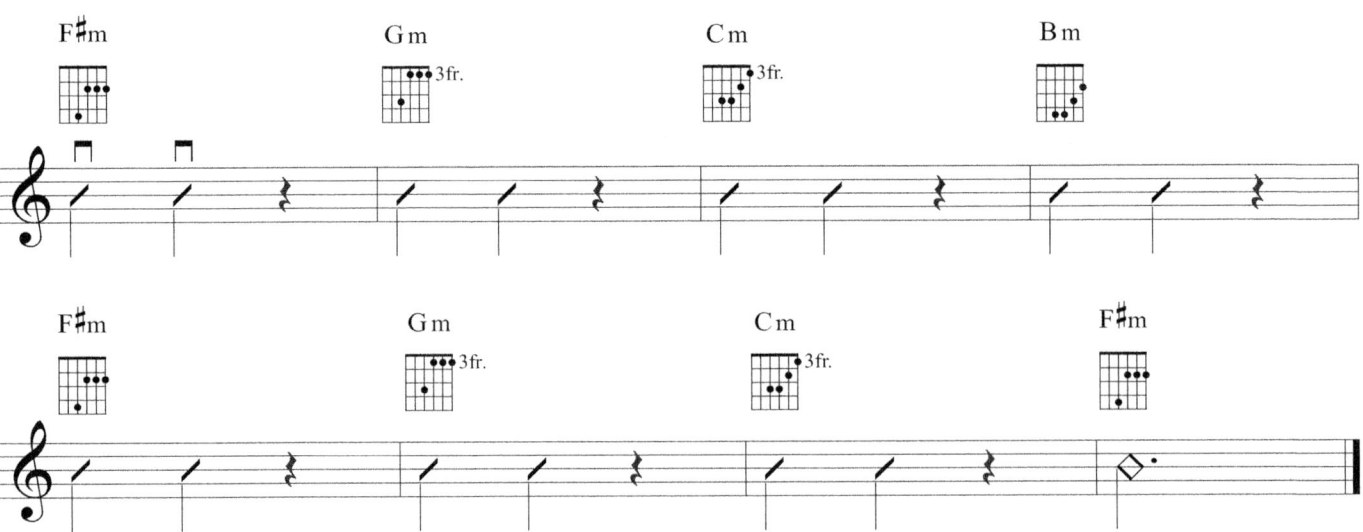

Lesson 20: Esus4 & Fsus4

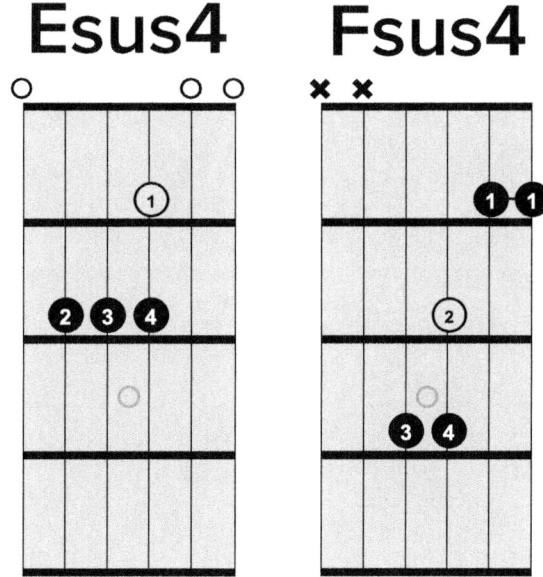

Try it: Practice the Esus4 and Fsus4 chords using the rhythms below.

Rhythm 1:

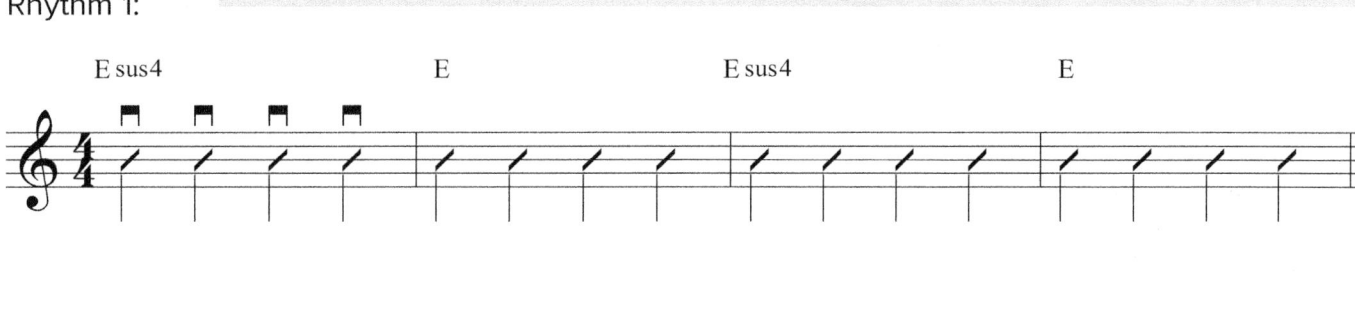

Rhythm 2:

Rhythm 3:

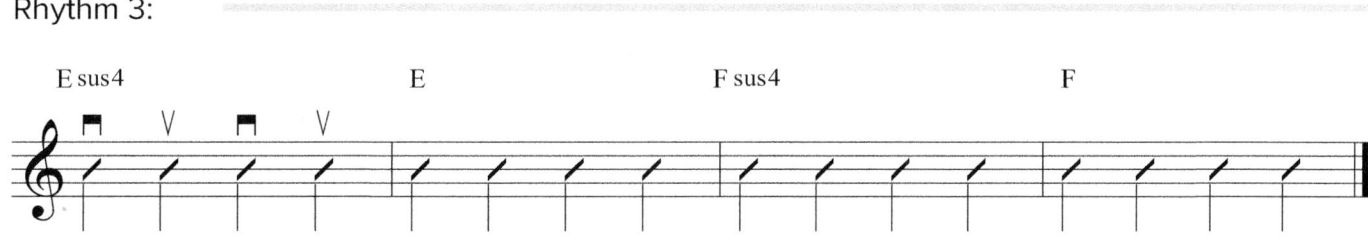

Practicing Esus4 & Fsus4

Exercise 1

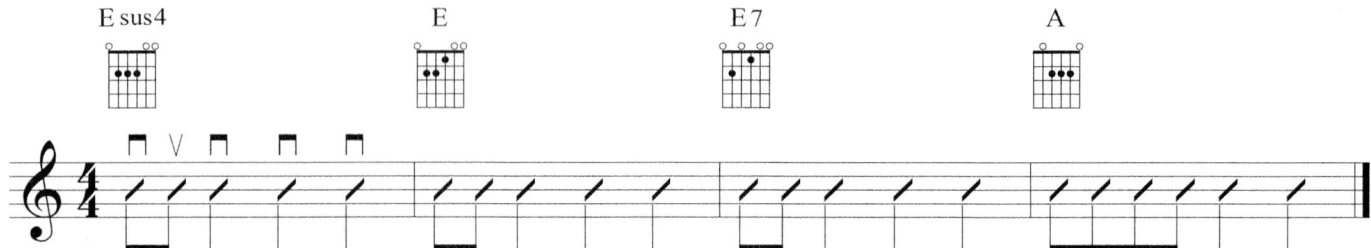

Exercise 2

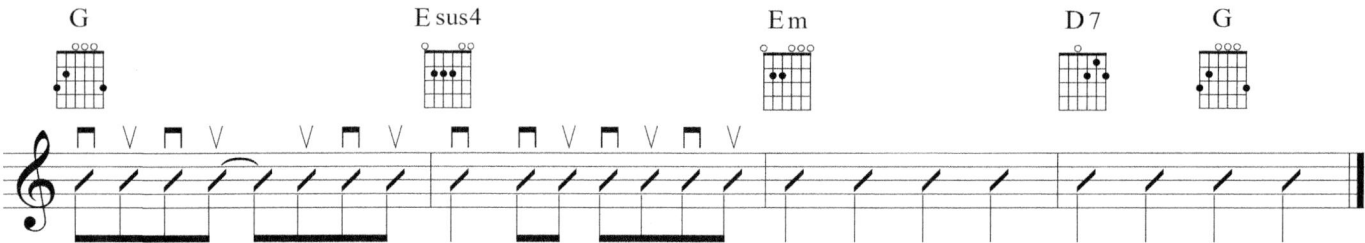

Exercise 3

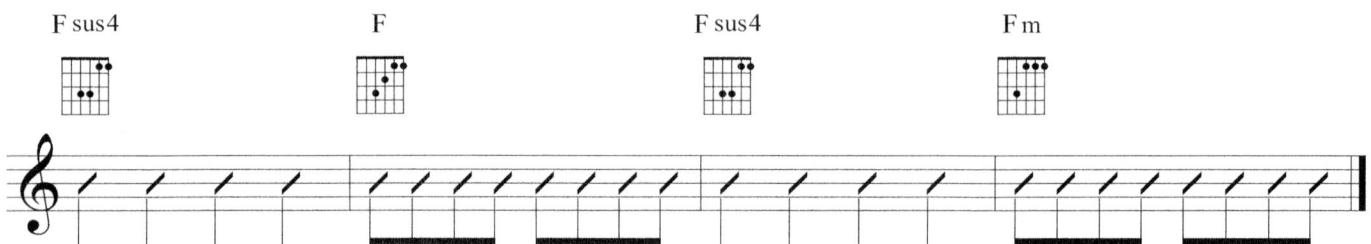

Exercise 4

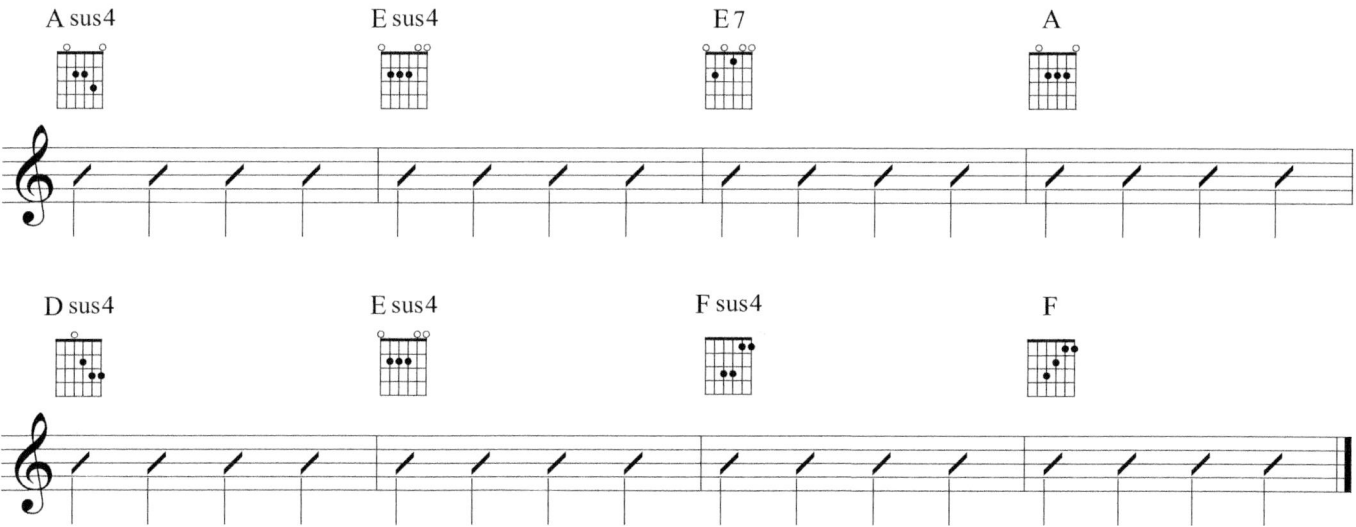

Exercise 5

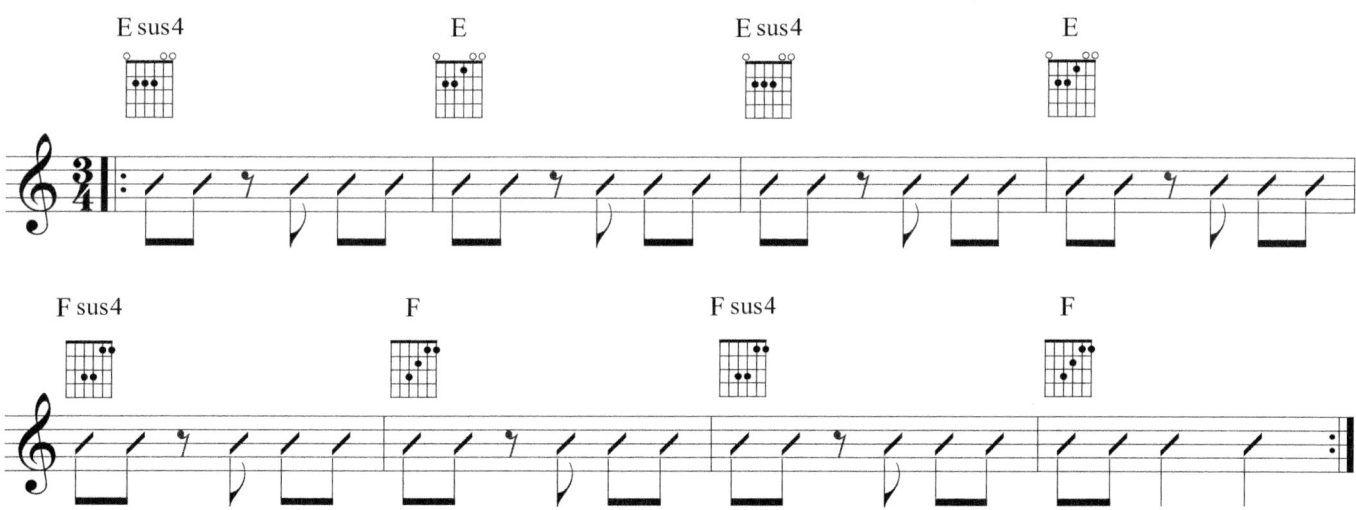

Summer

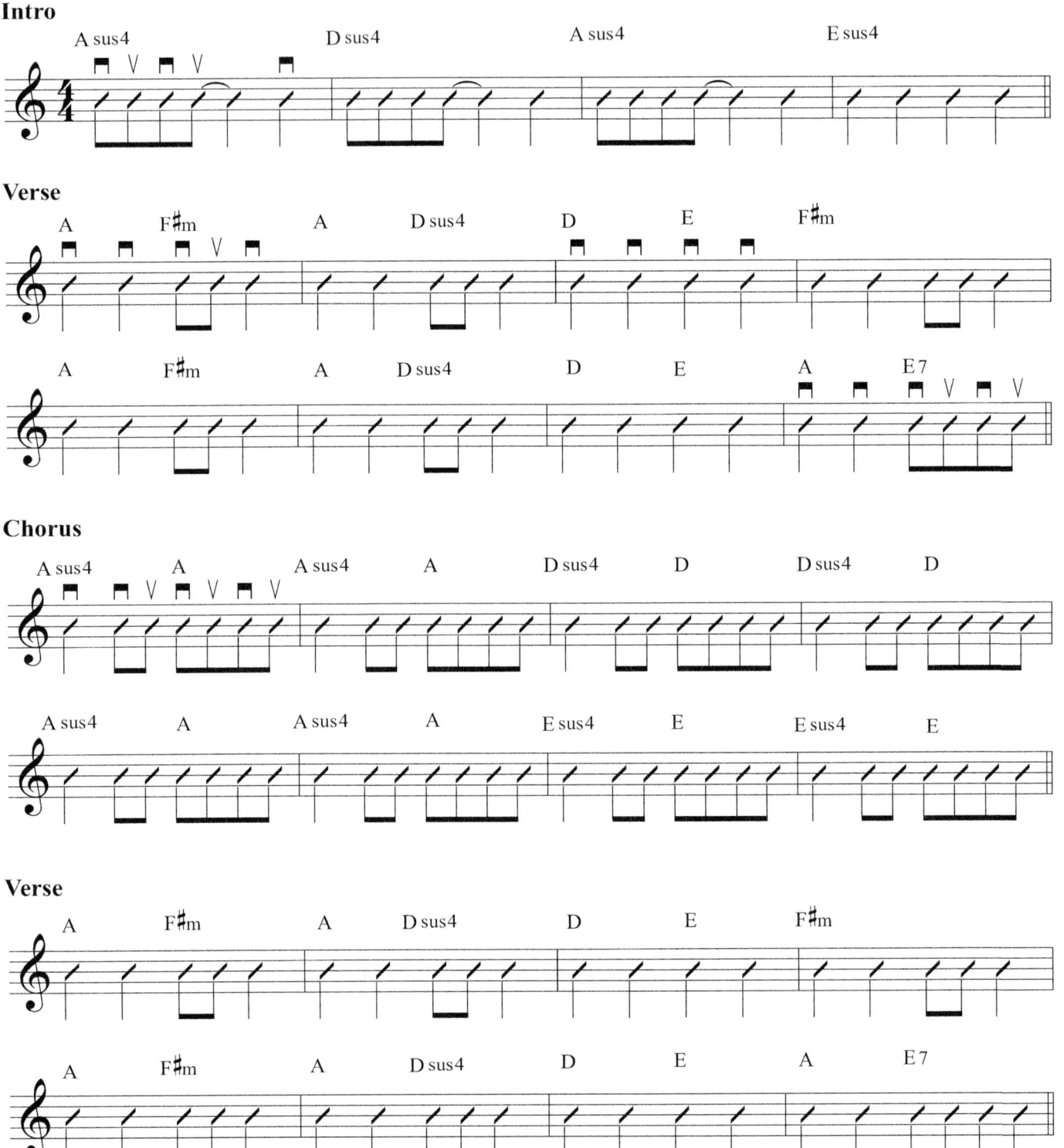

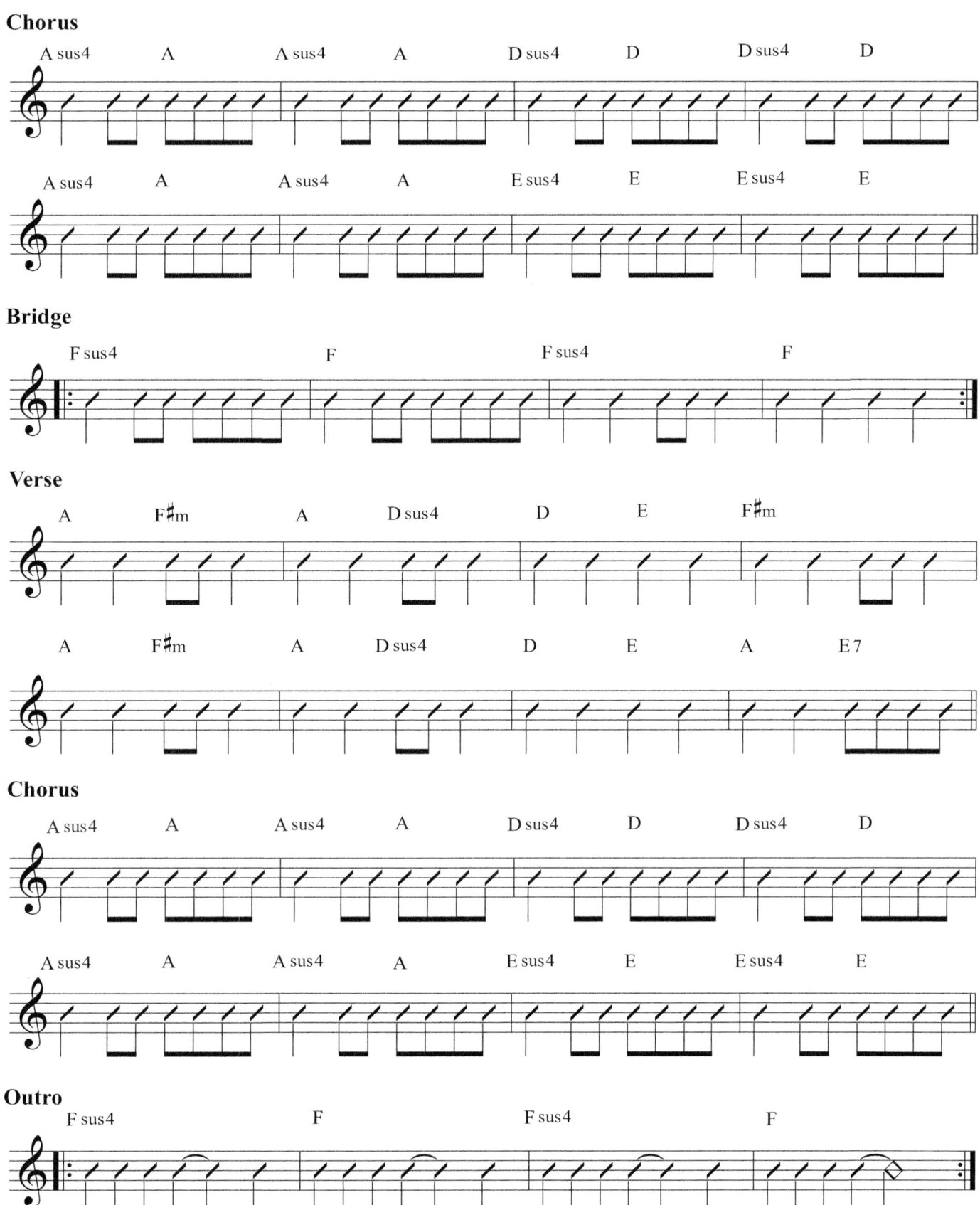

Not all songs use the Verse-Chorus-Verse-Bridge format. Early popular music, for example, used a song form called AABA. Each letter represents a section of music. Therefore, all the A sections will contain the same musical material, and the B section (often called the bridge) will contain contrasting material. Play the example below for a typical 32 measure AABA song.

Practicing AABA form

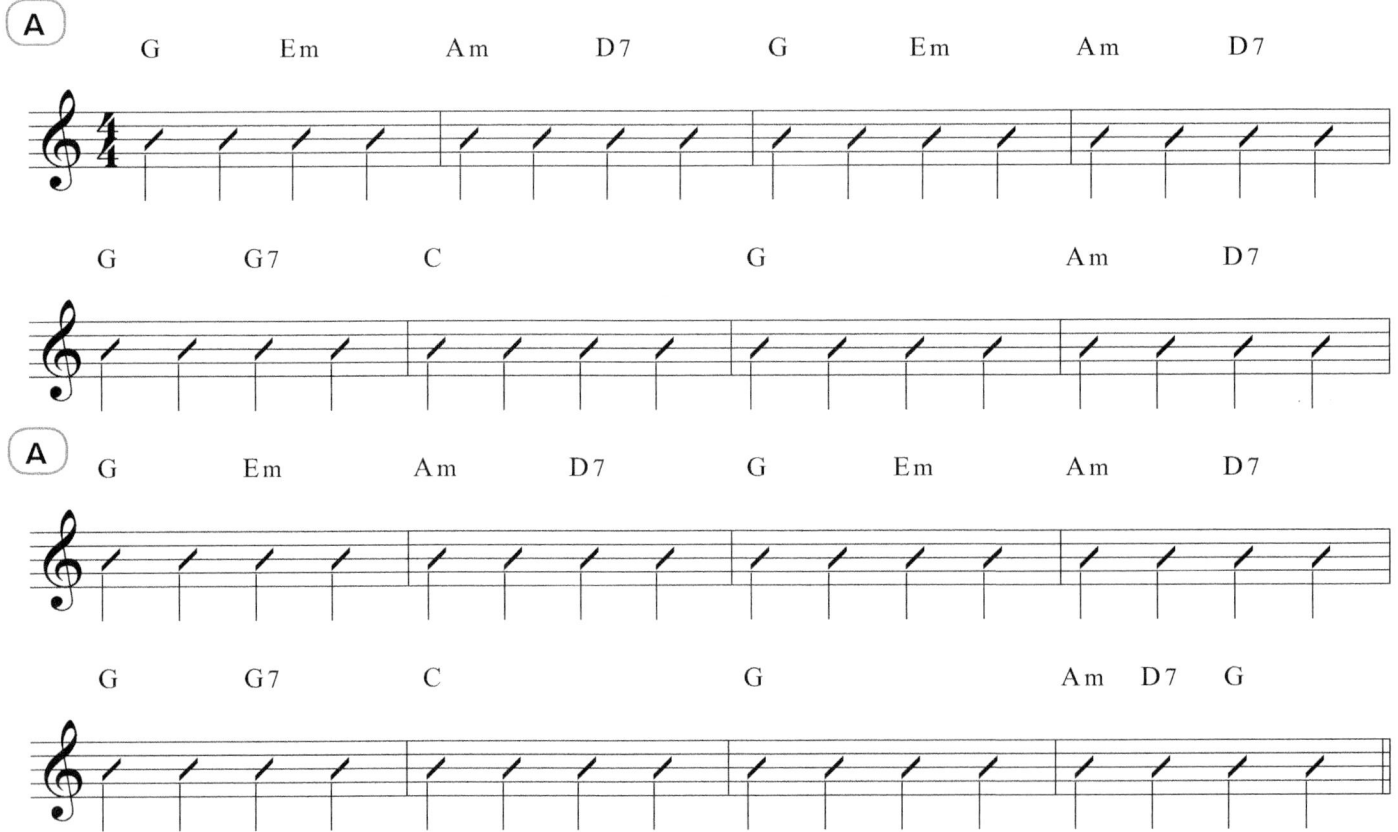

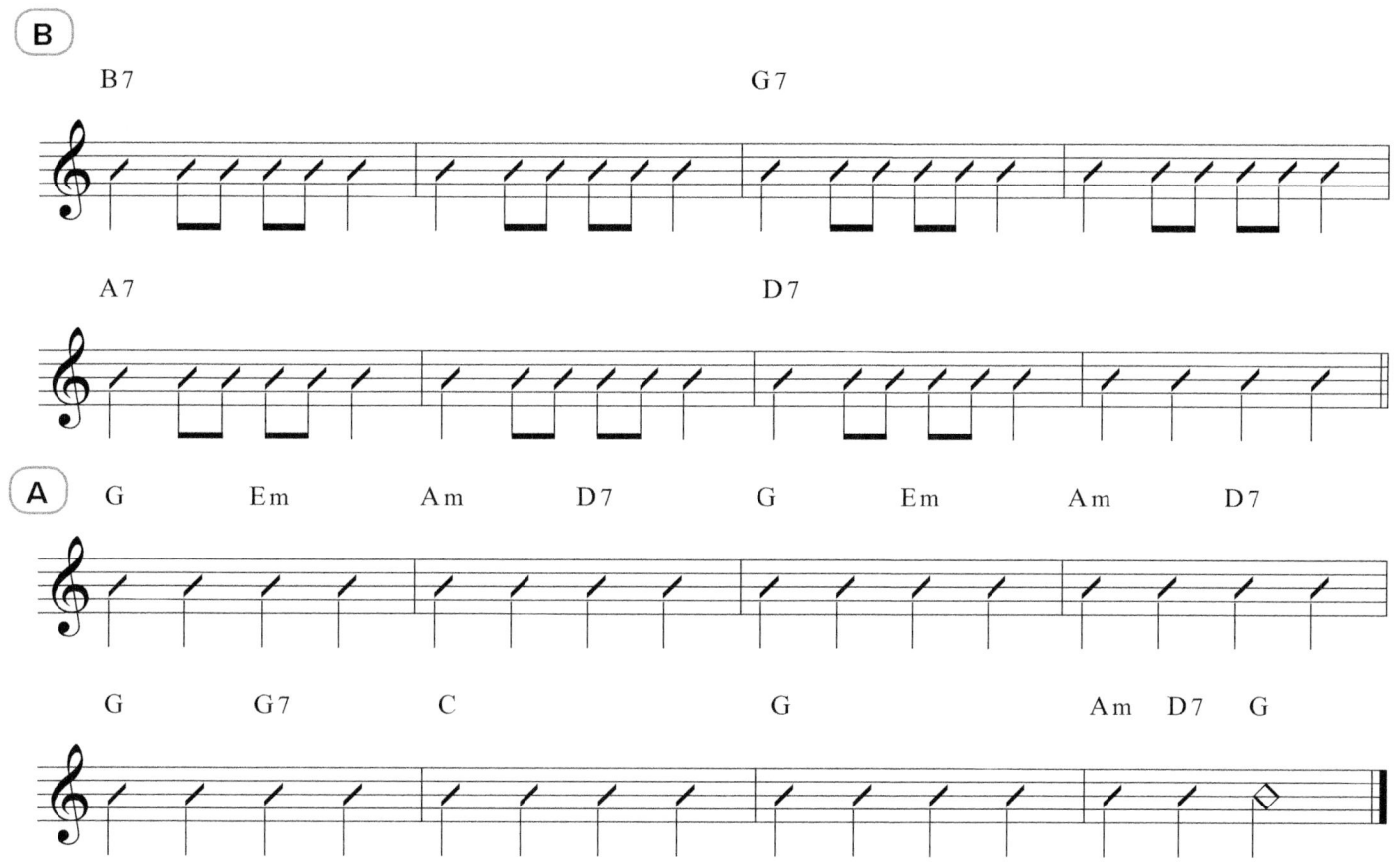

Willows and Pillows

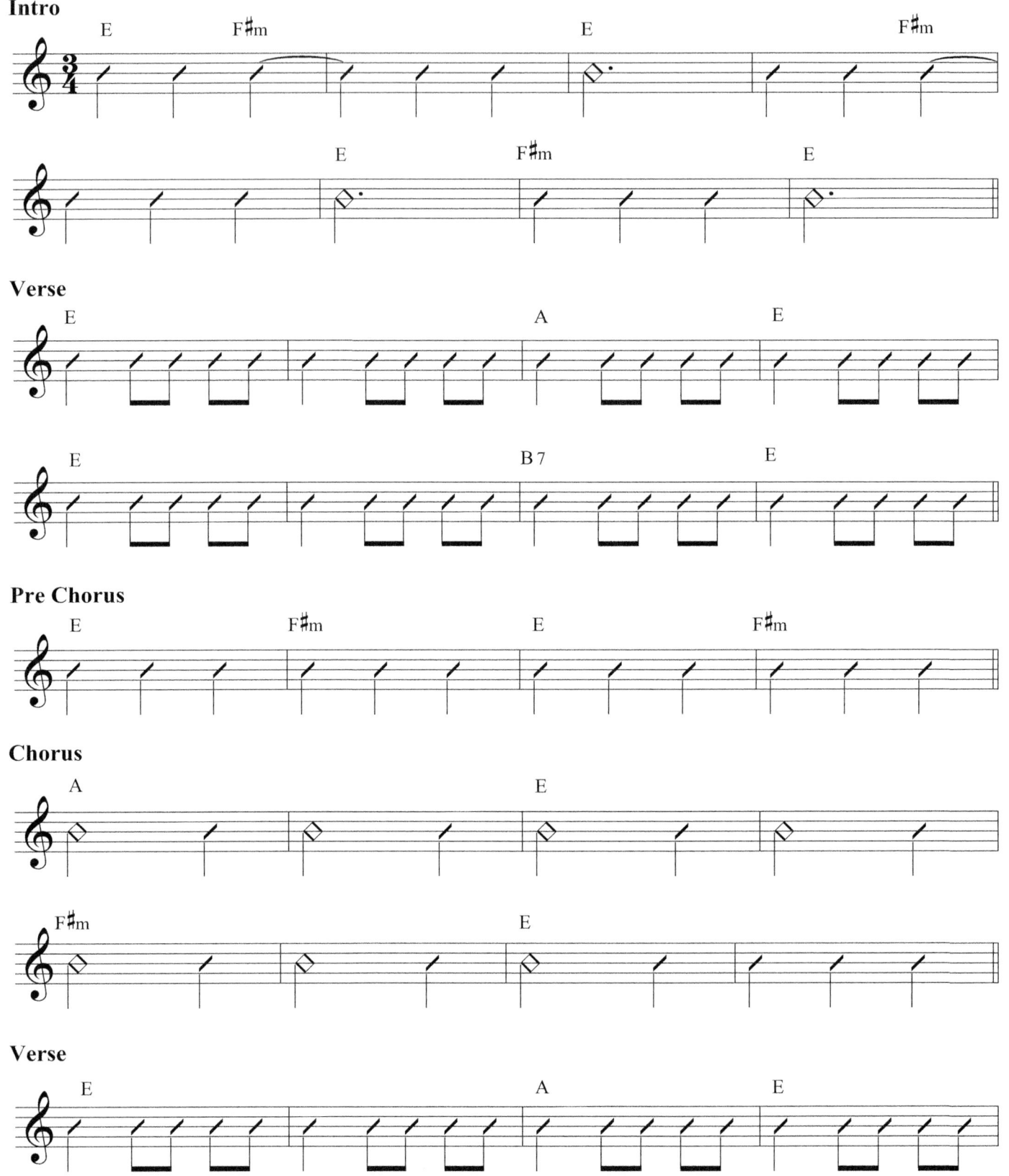

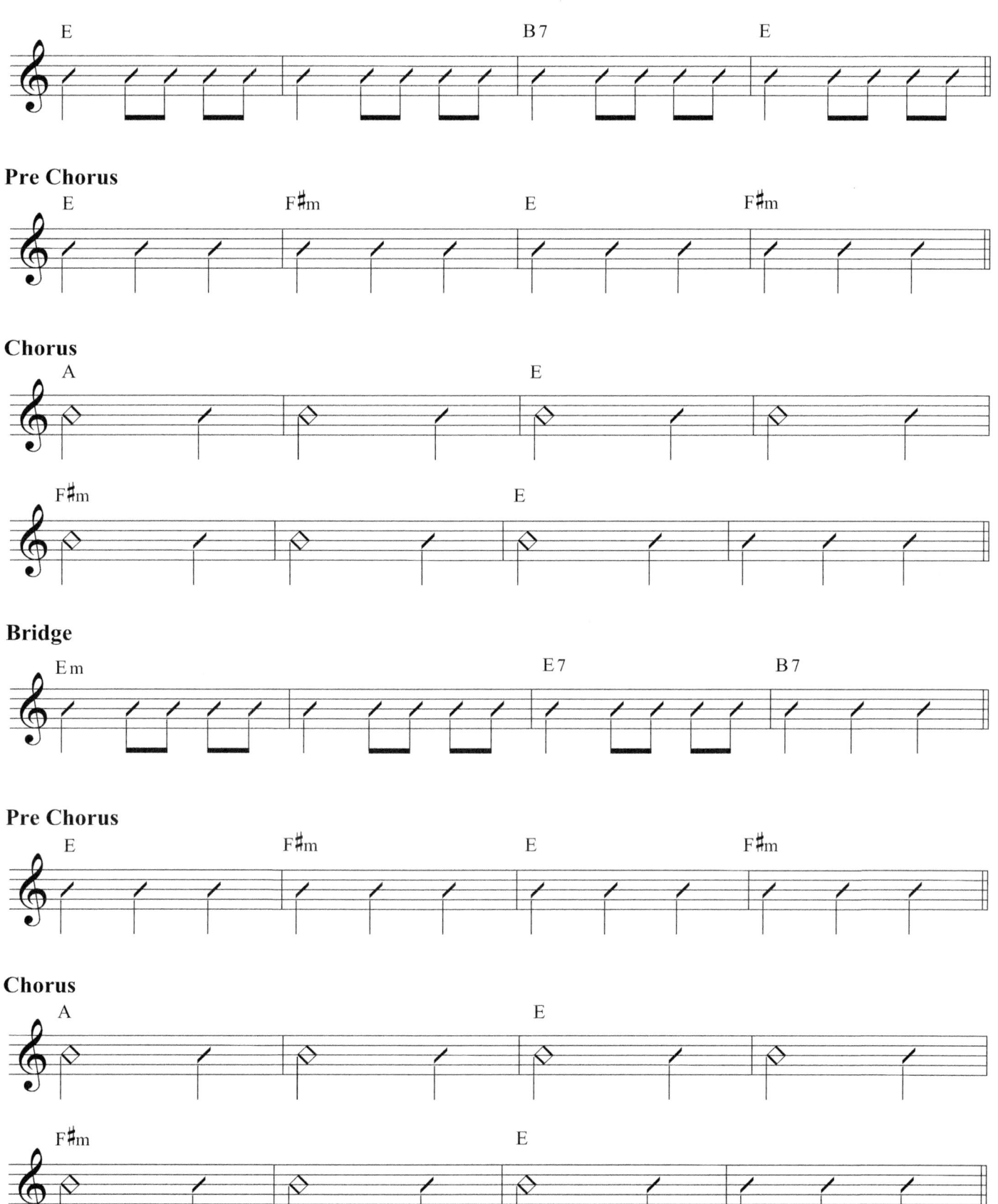

Outro

Most Triumphant

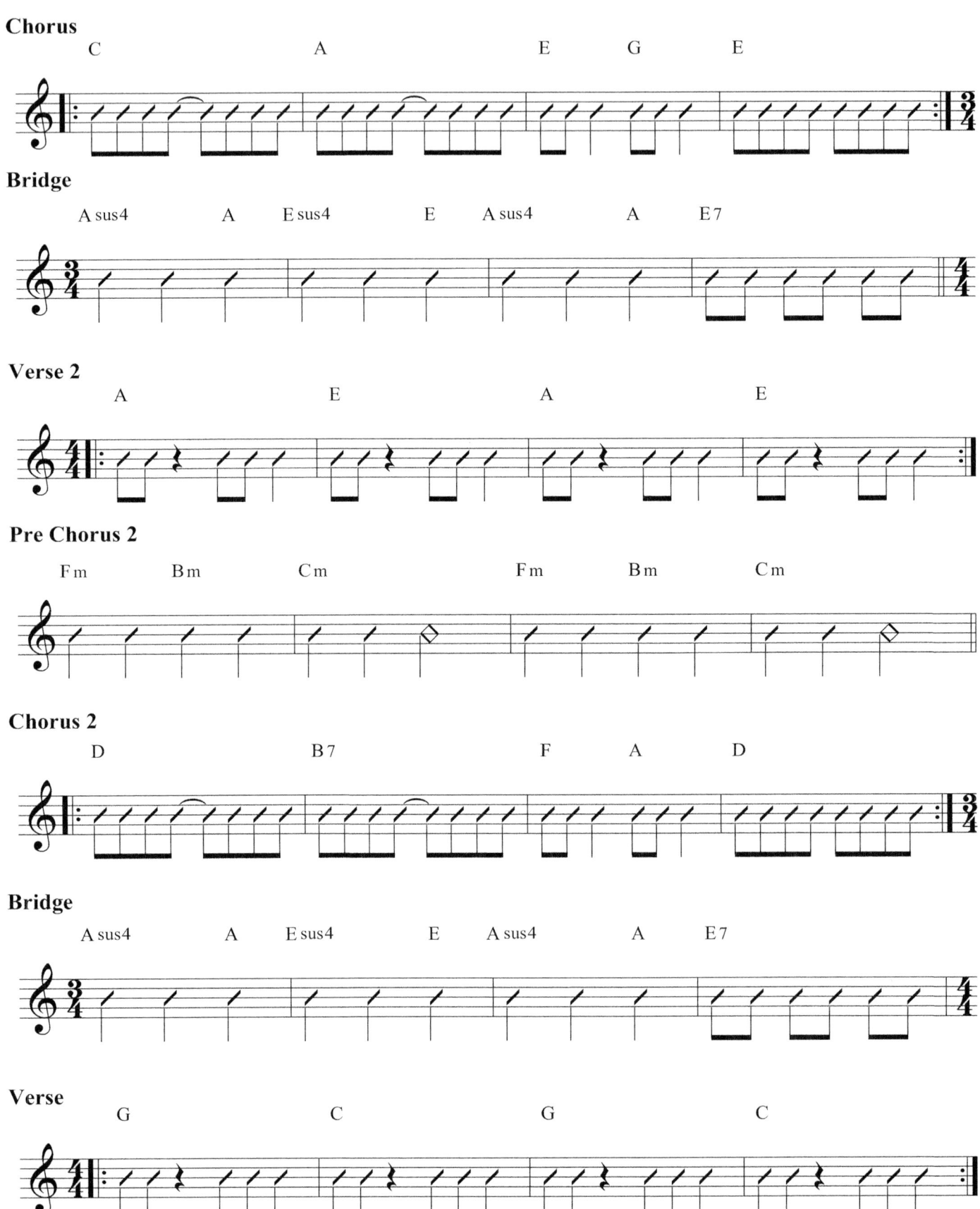

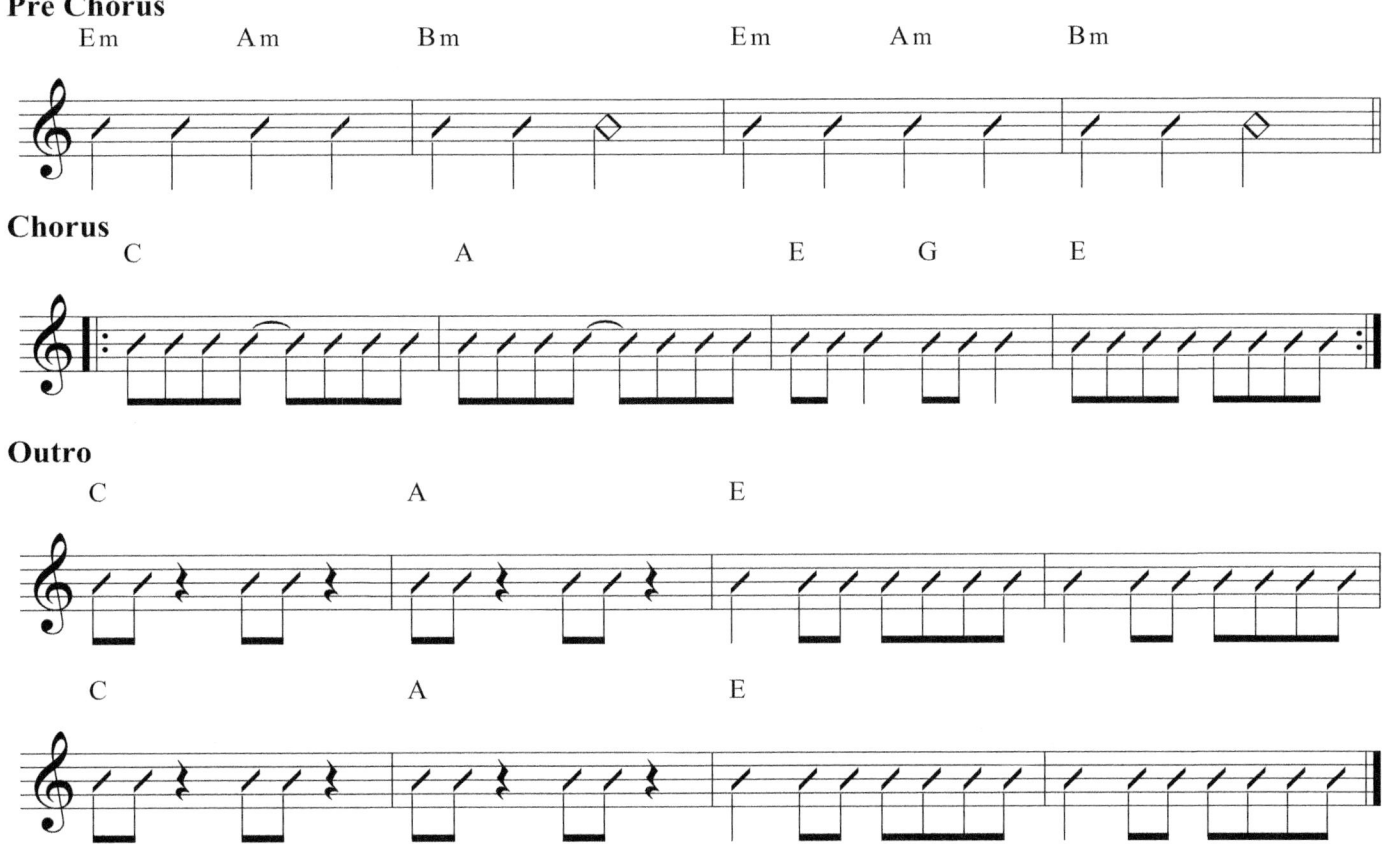

Chord Reference

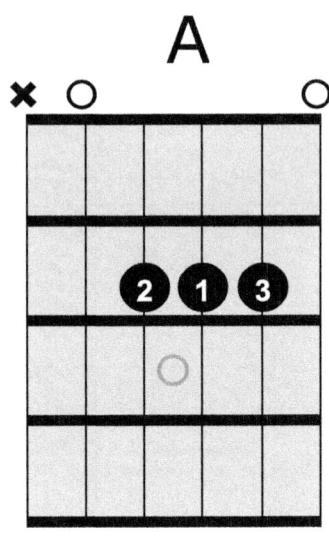
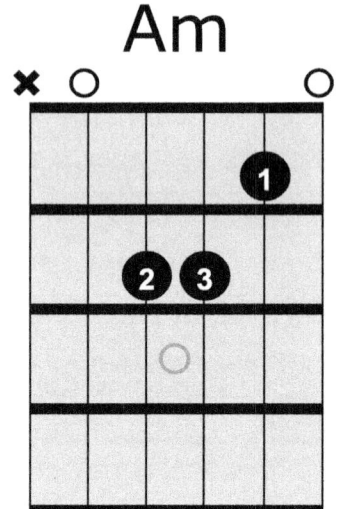
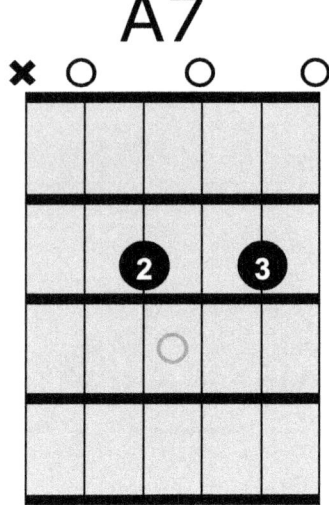
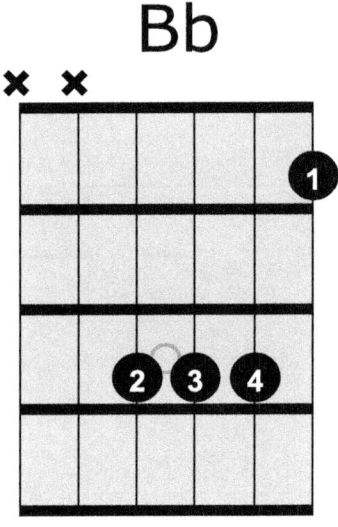
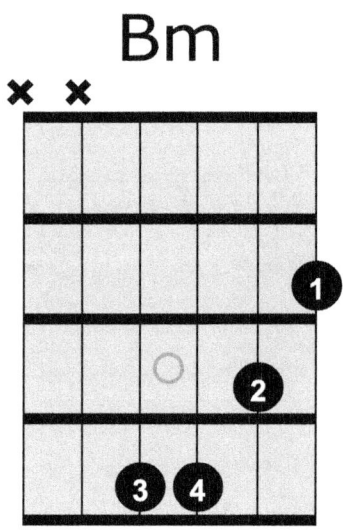
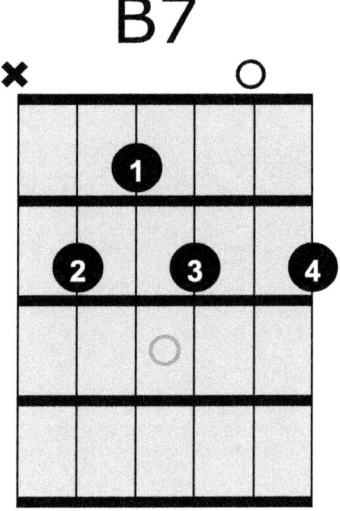
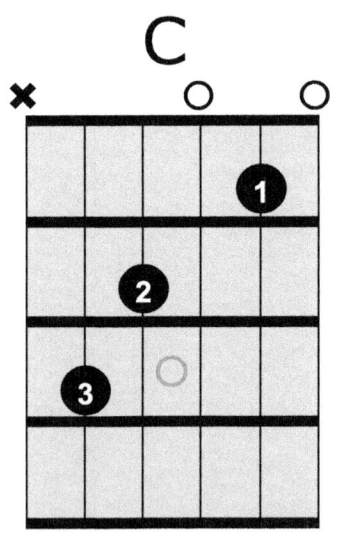
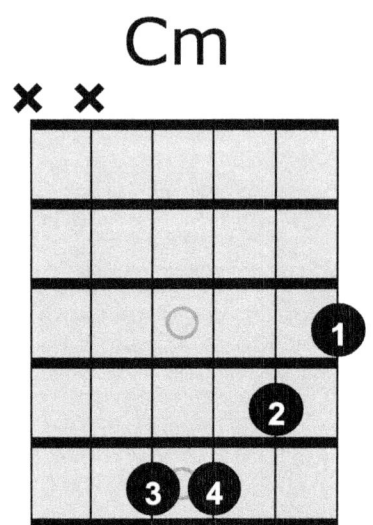
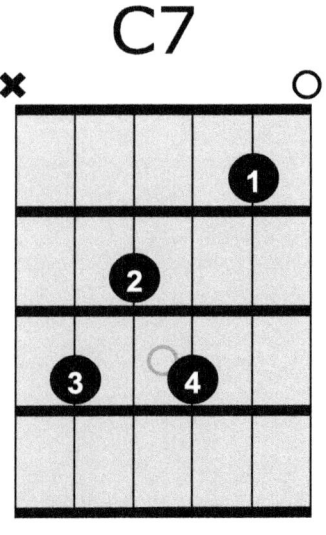

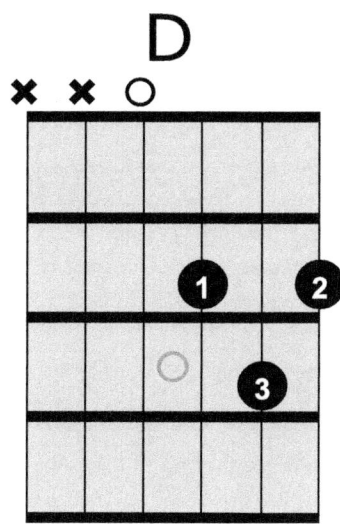
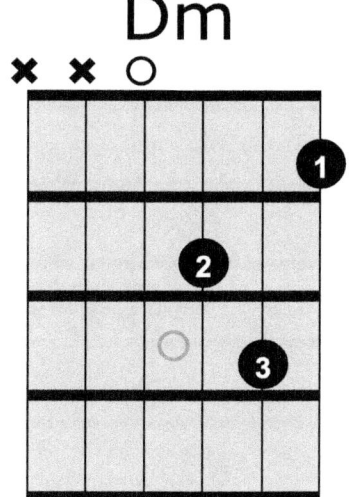
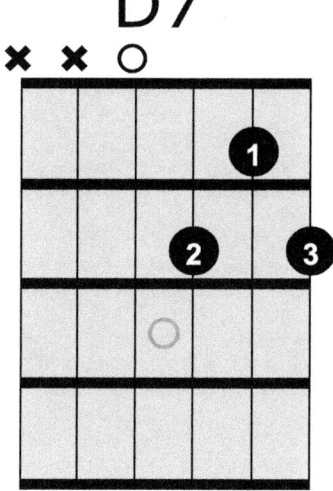
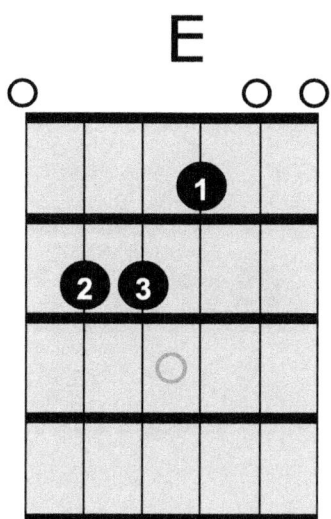
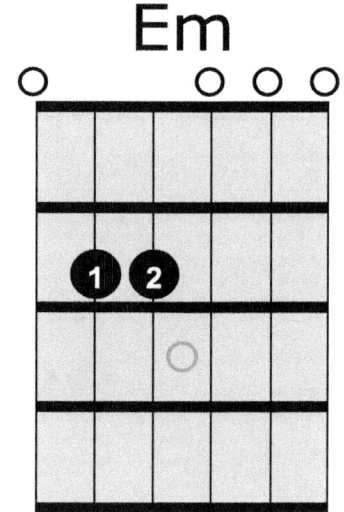
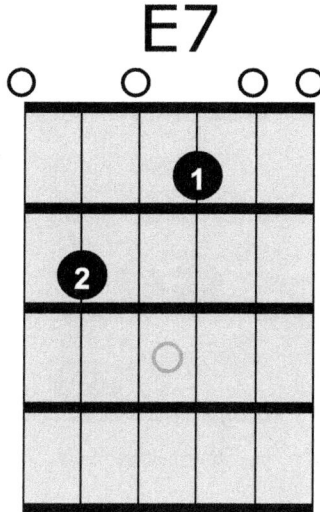
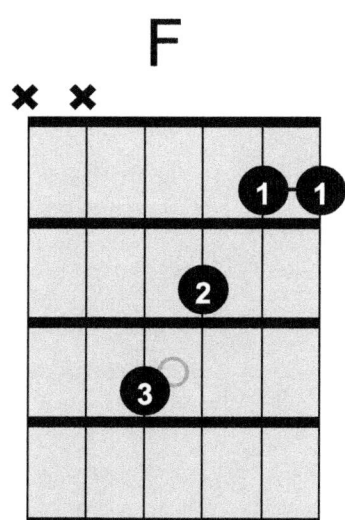
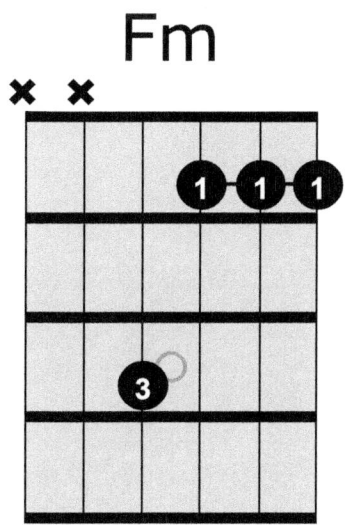
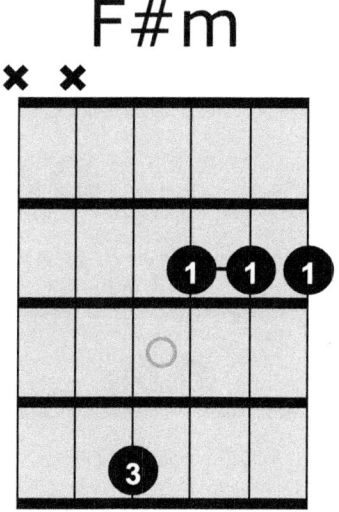

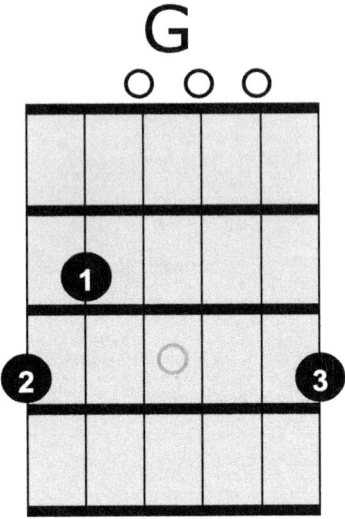
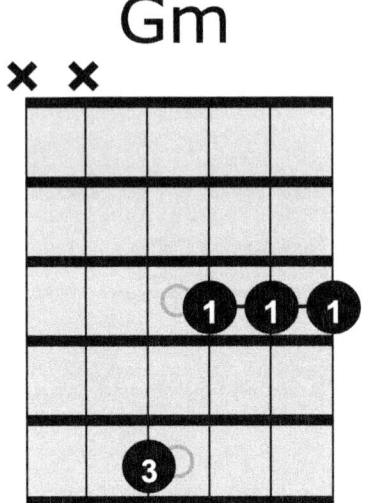
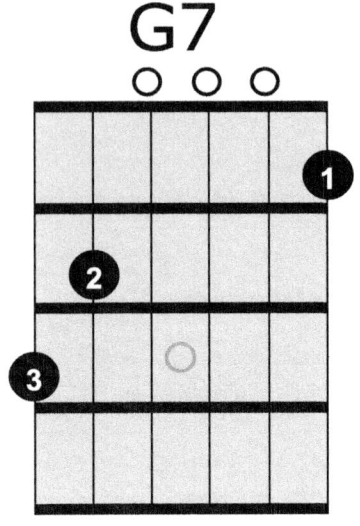
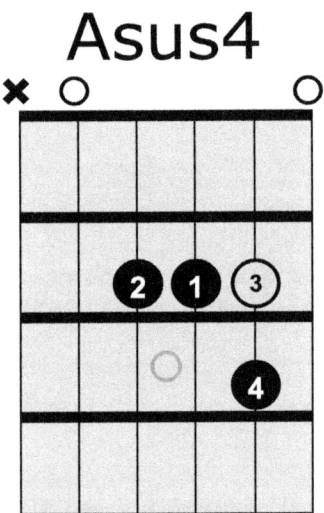
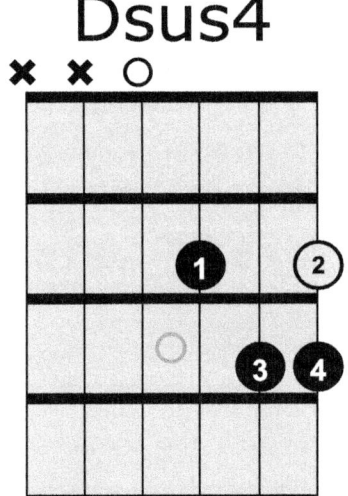
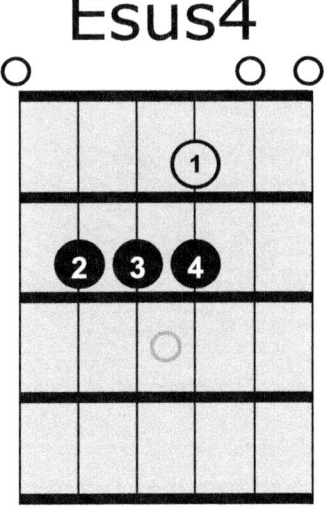
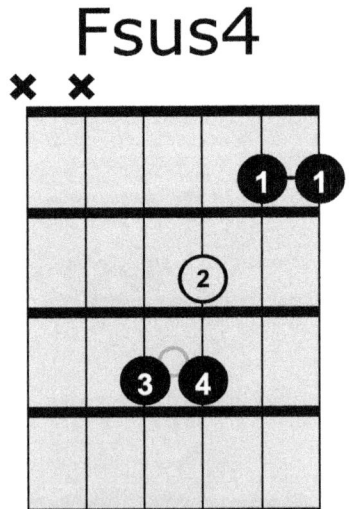

Resources to Take Your Playing Further

Guitar Chords Made Easy, Level 2: Beyond Basic Chords

With hundreds of practice exercises and example songs, Guitar Chords Made Easy Level 2: Beyond Basic Chords, takes your rhythm guitar playing to a whole new level. You'll learn how to strum more advanced chords such as maj7, m7, add9, 6s, and more. Not only that, but you'll also learn how to use a capo, play more advanced strum patterns, and start playing in compound time signatures, like 6/8. Available in right and left-handed editions.

Beginner Guitar

Now that you've conquered the basic chords, find out what else you can do with the guitar in *Beginner Guitar: The All-in-One Guide*. You'll learn note reading, review chords, learn how to read tablature, how to play a variety styles of music, fingerpicking, and much more, including guitar maintenance. Available in right and left-handed editions.

The Missing Method for Guitar Note Reading Series

Designed with the serious guitar player in mind, The Missing Method for Guitar Note Reading series teaches you how to read every note on the guitar, from the open strings to the 22nd fret. If you are looking to master the fretboard, this is the series for you! Available in right and left-handed editions.

Discover more at **TheMissingMethod.com**
facebook.com/TheMissingMethod
twitter.com/GuitarMethodTri

Index

A
AABA form 96

B
barre 57
barre chords 57
bars 7
beat 7
bridge 36

C
changing chords 10
chord, chords 1, 10, 11
  A7 25
  A Major 33
  A Minor 18
  Asus4 87
  B7 38
  barre chords 57
  B♭ Major 66
  B Minor 74
  C7 66
  C Major 18
  C Minor 74
  Common Chord Progressions 21
  D7 15
  D Major 25
  D Minor 44
  Dsus4 87
  E7 33
  E Major 38
  E Minor 12
  Esus4 91
  F Major 57
  F Minor 71
  F♯ Minor 84
  Fsus4 91
  G7 49
  G Major 12
  G minor 71
  minor barre chords 71
chord reference chart 104
chord symbols 11
chorus 23

D
dominant seven chords 11
  A7 25
  B7 38
  C7 66
  D7 15
  E7 33
dotted half note 62

E
eighth note strumming 28

F
flat 66
F major 57
four-four time 61

H
half note 7
harmony 1

I
introduction 47

M
major chord 11
measure, measures 7
meter 7
minor barre chords 71
minor chords 11
  Am 18
  Bm 74
  Cm 74
  D Minor 44
  Em 12
  Fm 71
  F♯ Minor 84
  Gm 71

N
notation 1

O
outro 51

P
pitch 7
pre chorus 54

Q
quarter note 7

R
repeat sign 30
rests 78
rhythm 7

S
sharp 84
Song Form 23
staff 7
strum, strumming 6
  eighth note strumming 28
  quarter note strum 28
  strumming with repeat signs 31
suspended chords 87
  Asus4 87
  Dsus4 87
  Esus4 91
  Fsus4 91

T
three-four time 61, 62
tie 77
time 7
  4/4 time 7, 61
  bars 7
  beat 7
  half note 7
  measure 7
  measures 7
  meter 7
  quarter note 7
  rhythm 7
  three-four time 61
  whole note 7
twelve bar blues 22

V
verse 23
visualization 10

W
whole note 7, 62

Printed in Great Britain
by Amazon